The first car race in Argentina was held on a racecourse in Buenos Aires ten years before Fangio's birth. In 1910, the Argentinean Automobile Club organised the first "Gran Premio de Carreteras" on the pebble-strewn dusty roads that snaked across the open spaces of that huge country. It was inspired by the town-to-town events held in France between 1895 and 1903 and linked Buenos Aires to Cordoba in the north. The winner was a certain Jean Cassoulet in an 18 hp De Dion Bouton who covered the 750 kilometres in a record time of 32 hours and 42 minutes. This event was the precursor of the road marathons that were to become an Argentinean speciality, in which, thirty years later, Fangio would show his extraordinary talent.

Argentina, Juan Manuel's birthplace, is a huge country (2 780 000 km^2 five times the size of France). According to the 1914 census there were only 7 885 000 inhabitants 30% of which were foreigners. Among the immigrants the Italians were the most numerous followed by the Spanish, Polish and Portuguese. The country's main riches came from its agriculture (cereals) and its beef, a staple food and also a valuable export. This increased between 1910 and 1920 as improved refrigeration techniques enabled it to be sent to increasingly distant markets, which required the construction of railways and roads.

Communications and transport have always been part of the nation's main preoccupations. In 1912, the country already had over 30 000 kms of railways whose building had been financed mostly by the banks and English companies. 70% of the traffic was made up of animals and cereals, which left little room for passengers! The road network was of poor quality for a long time, until the fifties in fact. A number of main roads between the principal towns consisted of paving stones and in periods of heavy rain became impassable.

For these reasons and also because of the low-income level of the general population the motorcar was slow to develop. In 1910, it was imported and thus a luxury reserved for a small minority which explains the fascination it exercised on Fangio's generation. In the ten years that followed Ford and Chevrolet set up strong dealer networks and then subsidiaries. The two big American companies had a virtual monopoly, as local construction was almost non-existent apart from makes like Buyatti and Gauchito. Thus Ford and Chevrolet were to play a preponderant role in Fangio's budding career.

The Argentina of his childhood was a fledgling democracy. It was initially attached to the vice royalty of Lima, thus under the yoke of Spain. Independence was declared in 1816 and a federal constitution was adopted in 1853 with Buenos Aires becoming capital in 1880. The next two decades were marked by the war against the Paraguayan Indians within the framework of the Triple Alliance with Brazil and Uruguay followed by the conquest of Patagonia. This territorial expansion led to the massacre of the Indian population and intensive cattle and sheep rearing created a dominant oligarchy, which held the reins of political power. In 1890, a brief popular revolt was put down with extreme severity. The economic problems that arose in the following decade (the country was over-reliant on its agriculture, cattle rearing and foreign investment) plus the political context led to profound changes. The power of the "estancieros" (the big landowners) was heavily curtailed and two new political parties emerged each with an anti-establishment programme: first of all the Radical Civic Union (later renamed the Radical party) and then in 1885 the Socialist Party. Both were created to protect the "new" Argentineans of European origin most of whom were in the low-income bracket.

● **3**_Juan Manuel's parents:
Don Loreto and Dona
Herminia Fangio.
(Christian Moity Archives)

Argentina also underwent a spectacular social evolution. The 1880s saw a rise of anticlerical feeling leading to the expulsion of the apostolic nuncio. Secularisation became the norm in the schools and civil marriages were recognised. Civil rights also progressed between 1900 and 1910 symbolised by the institution of the secret ballot (for men only) as women had to wait another 35 years to be given the right to vote! This law, initiated by the conservative president, Roque Saenz Pena, was pushed through the parliament in 1912 and changed the political landscape. In 1916, the Oligarchy lost the elections to the Radicals and a new president, Hipolito Irigoyen was elected: he remained in power until 1922 and again from 1928 to 1930. The 30s in Argentina were marked by the same political upheavals as in Europe but that's another story.

The next important date in Fangio's career was 1943 the year in which the president Ramon Castillo was thrown out of office. He was replaced by a junta made up of nationalist officers including the Minister of War, Juan Domingo Peron. Elected vice-president in 1944 he became president in 1946 a post that he held until 1955. Together with his second wife, the beautiful, glamorous and popular Eva Duarte affectionately known as Evita, he launched the "justicialiste" doctrine a curious mixture of nationalism, paternalism and socialism. He bought the railway network from the English and created a power base by flattering the aspirations of the workers and peasants either through concrete measures or electoral gimmicks. In the first case he gave women the right to vote and set up a very efficient social security system well ahead of the rest of Latin America; these measures were certainly advocated by Eva Peron. In the second, sport was privileged and as Peron himself was a passionate car lover motor racing leapt to prominence under his presidency.

At the height of his glory Juan Manuel Fangio never forgot his humble origins. He spoke of his father, Don Loreto, and his grandfather, Giuseppe, with tenderness and pride. The Fangios were part of the wave of Italian immigrants who came to Argentina at the end of the nineteenth century to populate and enrich the country. The family originated from Castiglione Messer Marino, a little village in the Chieta province in the Abruzzis. His grandfather, Giuseppe, left there in 1887 with a friend to seek his fortune in Argentina. The two men set out from Buenos Aires by train and then continued by road to reach the Los Padres Lake in the mountains on whose slopes trees grew in profusion. For three years Giuseppe worked in the charcoal industry and saved enough to buy ten hectares of land ten kilometres from Balcarce, still an agricultural village. It is 350 kilometres from Buenos Aires and 100 from Mar del Plata and was to become the Fangio's home. In 1891, Giuseppe returned to Italy and brought his wife and three children, Francisca, Alfonso and Loreto, to Argentina, the latter taking his precious accordion with him. The family lived a modest existence based around growing potatoes. Loreto spent his first three years in Argentina in Balcarce and when he was ten he went to live in Tres Arroyos some 200 kilometres southwest of his home town. He stayed there for three years and then returned to his family. His brother introduced him to a young girl who had been born in Tres Arroyos! She was of Italian origin as her parents originated from Tornarece some fifty kilometres from Castiglione Messer Marino in the province of Chiete. Her name was Herminia Deramo and she was two years his junior. They were married on 24th October 1903 and had six children: three daughters Carmen, Celia and Herminia and three sons José, Juan Manuel and Ruben nicknamed 'Toto' who became the future world champion's closest ally in the area of mechanics and in life in general. He helped him on his racing debut by tuning his cars and many years later when Juan Manuel retired "Toto" was there to help him install his car collection in the Balarce museum.

Juan Manuel Fangio was born in Balcarce on 24th June 1911 at 00h10. Loreto, a hard-working individual like his father, became a mason, plasterer and painter in the building trade. The little town was expanding so there was plenty of work around and soon he was able to buy a house for his family. It was located in a lively, popular quarter in 13th street named the "Steering Wheel" street as it was used by numerous lorries going to the station. An apt name for the childhood of a boy who was destined to become a world champion!

Juan Manuel had a happy childhood filled with games, swimming in a nearby lake, school (which he later said he liked very much especially maths) and evenings spent with his family. "We had no TV, not even a radio so we listened to dad telling us stories about our grandfather and his arrival in Argentina". Loreto also played the accordion but not when his wife was around, as she did not like music. Little did she imagine that one day Javier Mazzea would compose a tango based on her champion son! The song sung by Alberto Castillo was brought out by Odeon Records in 1949.

Fangio: you are the road champion
Fangio: you are king of the wheel
You are a man of great courage
Bandylegs, you can conquer all
With your masterly touch
Nothing can stop you

"Bandylegs" was the nickname that his classmates and football friends gave him. Juan Manuel was still at school when he discovered mechanical engineering, something that was to change his life. Aged eleven and a half he started a part time job at Francisco Cerri's who looked after carriages. A neighbour had a Carta (a make of car) powered by a single cylinder engine, which acted like a magnet for Fangio and his friends. He was taken on in the workshop of another Italian, Capettini, where he worked late into the night after school (he got up at 4 a.m. to study) as well as on Saturdays. It was there that he learned to drive a car, a chain-driven, Panhard et Levassor. Capettini left and Juan Manuel joined Carlini, who had a Rugby dealership, and also did a bit of racing. The first day he drove the racing Rugby with aluminium bodywork when going to visit a girlfriend in Tandil stuck in his memory. It was snowing, the roads were muddy and he was away for three days. It was the start of his racing apprenticeship. "You had to come into the corner at 60/70 km/h and exit at 100/110 km/h using the torque. You braked with the gearbox, never with the brakes because if they locked up the car became undriveable at the same time using the steering wheel and accelerator". This type of experience laid the basis of his driving style and twenty years later he would adapt it to post-war racing cars and tarred roads.

Juan's next job was with the Balcarce Ford agent, Estevez. The chief mechanic, Guillermo Spain, would become one of his teachers as well as a good friend. "At the start", remembers Juan Manuel, "my job was cleaning parts. And then bit-by-bit I was allowed to fit and adjust them. Parts were much more difficult to get than today so you had to be a bit of a blacksmith. When you didn't know what to do you watched those who did, and pinched their knowledge".

In 1924, Ford was assembling 45 000 cars and lorries in its Buenos Aires plant and another great American make, Studebaker, was about to invade Argentina. And in the Balcarce Studebaker agent's (Miguel Viggiano) workshop Juan Manuel became a highly skilled mechanic after mastering the art of adjustment. In addition, Viggiano tuned and drove racing cars as did one of his clients, Ayerza, who had already built up a bit of a reputation. Fangio was now aged sixteen and had given up school. Viggiano now trusted him enough to allow him to set up cars and adjust engines as well as delivering cars to Buenos Aires where he picked up new ones. In fact, Fangio did not have a driving licence and only passed it for the first time in his life in 1961 (3 years after his retirement) when on a trip to Brazil!

After a year Viggiano, who owed him several months back pay, gave him a present of an Indian (with a V2 engine) Harley Davidson's main rival. Juan, escorted by his boss in his car, tried out the bike on the road. Coming into a corner he changed down and the gearbox exploded! Viggiano then gave him a present of a 4-cylinder Overland which Juan quickly tuned for racing.

Suddenly things went all wrong for the 16-year-old Argentinean. He came down with pleurisy and was sick for a year. In those days when penicillin was not available it was a serious illness and could lead to tuberculosis. He grew thin. His mother was very worried and feared the worst. But he fought back courageously and modest as always he said later: "it was my friends coming to see me regularly who helped me get well". Finally, he recovered and after a final examination was declared fit to his great relief. History doesn't relate whether or not he was overjoyed about having to do his military service. But as he had almost died it was akin to a resurrection. He was able to start tough physical activities again and he threw himself into all kinds of sports including boxing, which he didn't like, football (the team was called 'Rivadavia; we'll come back to this name) and of course motor racing. ■

13

Chapter 2
1936-1938
First races

Chapter 3
1939–1942
"Carreteras Touring Cars"

● **8**_This is the 1939 Chevrolet Coupe in which Fangio cut his teeth in this form of racing on 19th and 20th October 1939 in the 'Gran Premio Argentino de Carreteras'. He came home 22nd.
(Museo del Automovilismo de Balcarce. William Huon archives)

● **9**_2nd April 1942. Fangio has just scored a victory on the Mar y Sierras road circuit in his Chevrolet Coupe 40. The flag at the finish is being waved by his friend and sponsor, Oscar Raul Rezusta. Note the name Balcarce painted on the side of the roof.
(Museo del Automovilismo de Balcarce – William Huon archives)

A wild, woolly, weird selection of around 120 vehicles entered for the events known as "Turismo de Carreteras" as they were based on series production American touring cars from 1937 to 1940. They were transformed, lightened and streamlined. The wings were pared down and bumpers, rear seats, cushions etc were removed or dismantled with the available space being used for an additional fuel tank, spare wheels and tools. The engines were boosted using all the tricks of the trade such as shaved cylinderheads, high compression pistons, large valves, high-lift camshafts, bigger carburettors, polished inlet and exhaust manifolds etc. Thus, a nice family Ford or Chevrolet (the dominant makes) was transformed into a roaring, snarling road rocket capable of over 160 km/h on the straight! The main problems were braking and road-holding due to the weight of the cars, their primitive design and high ground clearance, ladder chassis, rigid rear axles and leaf suspension. Despite improvements such as cooling vanes, scoops for the brakes and special shock absorbers it needed a large dose of courage (and perhaps a hint of folly) to set off at high speed with two people on board to go pedal to metal over stages of 700 or 800 km on roads strewn with pebbles which, when there was a storm, were quickly transformed into mud-covered tracks. Then once the drivers crossed the torrid and arid pampas, they had to tackle the Andes going up and down the mountains often at freezing altitudes on roads consisting of successions of hairpins and twists and turns bordered by precipices that would have struck terror in the heart of Sir Edmund Hillary himself!

The "Gran Premio de Carreteras" was a hodgepodge of endurance, speed, rallying and stock car racing that demanded of the drivers, navigators and mechanics a dauntless spirit allied to refined skills, physical endurance, anticipation and improvisation. Luck too played a part. And as if this was not enough the races took place in an ambience of popular frenzy with spectators whose discipline was not their strong point, massed on either side of the road on the entry and exit of the stage towns. At strategic points along the itinerary well-placed loud speakers and radios broadcast the latest news at full blast. This was the school in which Fangio honed his skills and became a legend in his own country before tackling the international scene.

In 1939, after a circuit event in May Juan Manuel opted for the road races, which, at that time in Argentina, were the most prestigious and the best way to make a name for himself. In 1938, two drivers from Buenos Aires, the Galvez brothers, Oscar the elder and Juan the younger made their debut in the "Gran Premio Argentino" in a V8 Ford coupe, the quickest car of the era. Fangio's good friend, Oscar Raul Rezusta, launched a subscription for him in Balcarce and 240 of his friends dug into their pockets. He was looking for the same car as the Galvez brothers and not finding one chose a Chevrolet instead which he bought from the make's agent. It was a new coupe painted black with a straight 6-cylinder overhead valve engine but was less powerful than the V8 side valve Ford. He did all the tuning himself.

In his first race the "Gran Premio Argentino de Carretera" run on 19th-20th October he came home a disappointing twenty-second hindered by lubrication problems caused by the design of the engine. After revising the lubrication system he turned up for the next major event, the "Gran Premio Extraordinario", held between 29th October and 25th November. His mechanic and navigator was Hector Carlos Tieri. Several stages were cancelled because of storms, which made the roads impassable, and the cars were transported by train. When the race restarted Fangio clawed his way up from the back of the field and led for a brief period until he made a slight error and went off. The Galvez brothers retook first place and drove on to victory while Juan Manuel fought his way back to finish fifth overall. After this the Argentinean public split up into "Galvistas" and "Fangistas", country versus city, Ford against Chevrolet. The men in charge of General Motors, who had ignored Fangio's private effort, while entering a works car, provided him with assistance and tyres as the finish approached. Despite his result he still had debts and after the race he sold his car to pay them off.

Fangio and his fans got their revenge during the 1940 season especially as the major event assumed even greater importance. The organisers decided to promote the future Pan-American highway, rebaptised the event "Gran Premio del Norte" and extended both its length and duration: 9441 kilometres over fifteen days between 27th September and 12th October from Buenos Aires to Lima and back by way of Bolivia which entailed crossing the Andes. It was a truly extraordinary race and Fangio won it easily in his Chevrolet although physical exhaustion and vertigo threatened himself and his co-driver. They had to chew coco leaves and garlic to keep going! Juan Manuel said later that he came close to plunging into a ravine on several occasions. The route was long and as hard on cars as on their drivers and he was up against tough opposition like the Galvez brothers, Ernesto Hilario Blanco, Angel Lo Valvo all previous winners of the race and former Argentinean champions. There were only 32 survivors. Fangio received over 20 000 pesos in prize money for overall victory plus stage wins. This sum enabled him to buy the car, settle a few debts and then finance the construction of the new service station in Balcarce. On 14th December he raced in the Argentinean Thousand Miles and finished eighth winning his first Argentinean Championship title in the category.

He really made his name in 1941. Argentina was not yet hit by the effect of the war raging in Europe and carried on as if nothing had happened. It was the same in Brazil where the Gran Premio Presidente Getulio Vargas was held from 22nd to 29th June over a 3 900 km itinerary made up of seven stages crossing the Minas, Gerais, Goya and San Paolo provinces. Fangio and Oscar Galvez were invited as Argentinean champions. They travelled together, shared a room to save money but each one prepared his car in his own way without receiving any help from either Ford or General Motors. Before the start Fangio had new bearings fitted to his Chevrolet coupe in secret in a workshop in Rio de Janeiro owned by two white Russians. He told them that he did not have enough money to pay as he had spent his last pesos at the end of his journey from Balcarce by road. "Don't worry about it, you can settle up after the race. We know that you're going to win", was their reply!

And Fangio did not disappoint them. He won three stages with his new navigator, Vasco Elizalde. Oscar Galvez came home first in the other three and only the second-last escaped the Argentineans due to a navigational error. Juan Manuel finished so far ahead of Galvez that he had enough time to wave the chequered flag to his fellow-countryman! Thanks to the large cash prize awarded to the winner he was able to return home by steamer. However, before boarding the 'Brazil' he paid his mechanics and held a party in their workshop. He arrived in Buenos Aires on 9th July. In December he won the Thousand Miles and was crowned Argentinean champion for the second year running. However, the big surprise in this event was the performance of Oscar Galvez's younger brother Juan making his racing debut, who came home second behind Fangio.

Despite rumours of petrol rationing in Argentina as the war spread the "Gran Premio del Sur" was held between 21st January and 3rd February 1942. Fangio was at the start in the village of Mercedes in the province of Buenos Aires. The race in ten stages went right down to Patagonia where it crossed into Chilean territory. It was a very tough event for Juan Manuel and Elizalde as they were hit by a raft of mechanical problems. A bearing punctured the sump and they had to do a soldering job using aluminium from a saucepan as well as repairing a broken windscreen with glass cut from a side window! They finally came home tenth out of 14 survivors after 7 200 kms of sheer hell.

By now Argentina was starting to feel the pinch. The government brought in war measures such as the sale of maize for fuel and tyre restrictions for both lorries and private cars; on 2nd April the final "pre-war" road race, won by Fangio again, was held on the Mar y Sierras circuit. A few more circuit events were held in the spring but almost five years would elapse before Juan Manuel would race again: February 1947 to be exact. The wait seemed interminable for him. He survived in Balcarce by selling lorries or their tyres. On roads that were deserted by traffic he studied and refined his techniques in the areas of braking and cornering on his delivery runs to clients hoping that one day they would come in useful. ∎

● **10**_In 1947, Fangio started racing again in this model T Ford heavily modified by Nardi (no relation to the Italian of the same name) on the La Pomona circuit in San Just in the Fomenta Limitad category reserved for Model T. *(Museo del Automovilismo de Balcarce – William Huon archives)*

Chapter 4
1947-1948
Triumph and tragedy

● **11**_Rosarrio 1st May 1947:
Juan Manuel Fangio victorious
in his "Negrita", a single-seater
eligible for the Mecanica
Nacional category. It consisted
of a Chevrolet engine in a
Ford T chassis and was tuned
by his brother Ruben 'Toto'
Fangio.
*(Museo del Automovilisimo de
Balcarce – William Huon
archives)*

General Juan Domingo Peron became Argentinean president on 26th February 1946 and took over power in June. From his point of view racing represented a source of prestige and power for his country so he organised a programme of events called the Temporada with the Argentinean Automobile Club for the start of 1947, a sporting season in the southern hemisphere open to different forms of racing. Constructors like the Orsi brothers (Maserati) were contacted as well as famous European drivers. Transport for both them and their cars would be paid for as well as luxurious hotels. Fantastic parties would be laid on and good starting money paid on one condition, each team would provide a car for a local driver. These would be chosen by the Automobile Club and after the test, the most promising would be sent to race in Europe with financial help from the government.

At the end of 1946 Fangio was not yet in a position to benefit from Peron's scheme. He was looking for a car capable of racing in the newly created "Mecanica Nacional" category. The choice was limited even though foreign cars were allowed to race provided that they had been assembled in Argentina. Most of the makes were American like the Ford T chassis that was hidden

away in a corner of the workshop in Balcarce. 'Toto' his younger brother helped by José Duffard shoehorned a 4-cylinder Chevrolet into it and did the tuning. And so the "Negrita" (little black one) as the Fangio brothers called became Juan Manuel's vehicle for the restart of racing in Argentina and coincided with his own rise to fame as a driver.

The Temporada began on 15th February with the Buenos Aires Grand Prix. Fangio was entered in the Formula Libre category and so caught up was he in taming his recalcitrant single-seater that he had no time to see the invited stars like Villoresi and Varzi, shooting past in their Maseratis. On 1st March he won the "Mecanica Nacional" class on the Rosario circuit and finished sixth in the International category. The field consisted mainly of pre-war models among which were Maseratis and supercharged Alfa Romeos. He retired at Necochea and on 20th April he came third on the Mendoza circuit in the "Mecanica Nacional" Category.

Fangio had just turned thirty-six and realised that he had little time left to make a name for himself. He bought an Argentinean car, a Volpi (nothing to do with Count Volpi, the founder of the Scuderia Serenissima in Venice). It was a real racing car powered by an American

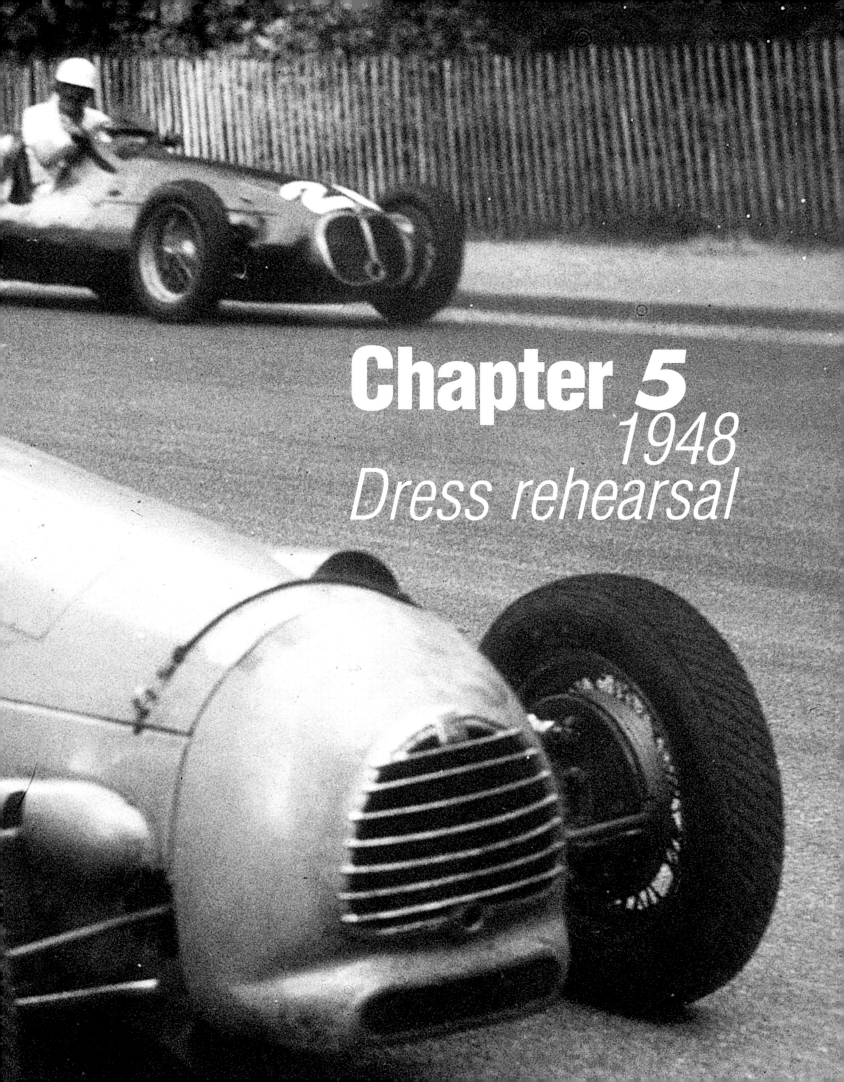

Chapter 5
1948
Dress rehearsal

1948 would have been a good season for Fangio were it not for the tragedy in the Andes. It was the year of his real circuit-racing debut. In January 1948 during the second Temporada organised by the Argentineans he was given a drive in not one but two of the European racing cars that had made the trip: a 1500 cc Maserati and an 1100 cc Simca-Gordini. A member of the Argentinean Automobile Club bureau tells the following story that was typical of the man: "All the Argentinean drivers who came to see us to discuss a possible drive in one of these cars all asked the same question sooner or later. 'How much will I be paid?' Fangio asked: 'How much is it going to cost me?' We chose him right away!"

Of course, Fangio got paid, as the ACA selection committee, including the very knowledgeable Francisco Borgonovo, knew how talented he was. His career was about to take off!

The new International Racing Formula no.1 had just been drawn up by the CSI (International Sporting Commission), the sporting branch of the FIA for the 1947 season. The F1 Championship for Drivers did not start until 1950 but from now on the main Grands Prix were run to Formula 1 regulations. However, the Argentinean Temporada was an exception as there were events for "Coches Especiales" a Formule Libre that accepted pre-1940 Grand Prix cars or the new F1s.

On 17th January Achille Varzi, the great Italian driver, was at the wheel of a big 4.5 litre V12 Alfa Romeo for the "Premio Ciudad de Buenos Aires" held in the Palermo Park, a kind of Bois de Boulogne in the centre of the city. Luigi Villoresi still had not got his hands on the new 4 CLT/48 Maserati and had to content himself with a 4 CL (a supercharged 1500 cc version built for the pre-war Voiturette Formula) as did Ruggeri and Platé driving for the Scuderia Milano which entrusted a 3litre 8 CL to Nino Farina. Amédée Gordini, the French constructor of Italian origin, brought along a pair of 1100 cc Simca-Gordinis one of which was for Jean-Pierre Wimille, one of the greatest French drivers, under contract to Alfa Romeo which did not race in the Temporada. A brief but intense friendship was to blossom between the French veteran and the Argentinean newcomer.

That day marked Fangio's debut at the wheel of a European single-seater, one of the two 4 CL Maseratis entered by the French team, Naphtra Corse set up by "Raph" whose real name was Raphaël de Montbressieux. He was an independent French driver of Argentinean origin on his mother's side (de Las Casas) and drove the other 4 CL while Oscar Galvez, Fangio's eternal rival, selected by the ACA entered his own 8 C 35 Alfa Romeo.

To everybody's surprise Fangio was third quickest in practice and found himself on the front row alongside Villoresi in front of 100 000 delirious fans. He held on to fourth place until lap 4 when the gear lever came away in his hand! Eight days later in Mar del Plata he finished fifth in the Maserati. His intrinsic skills - calmness and determination, capacity to adapt, precision in cornering - had already caught the eye of the top drivers including Achille Varzi, who loved Argentina and he advised Fangio to go and race in Europe. And of course, Jean-Pierre Wimille as according to Olivier Merlin the Frenchman had attended the Tres Arroyos 400 km race in 1938 and spoke about Fangio on his return to France. His boss at the time Amédée Gordini also recognized talent when he saw it as Christian Huet related. In Rosario on 1st February Fangio joined Wimille in the Simca-Gordini squad in the second car. The Frenchman did not know the circuit and during practice Fangio showed him the way round and lapped 1.5s quicker than the Frenchman. The next day they were battling for the lead until the Argentinean's car was slowed by a split cylinderhead. On 14th February they were back racing on the Palermo park track and this time Juan Manuel finished in a lowly eighth place in both events. Wimille, however, was unstinting in his praise of Fangio as he realised just how good he was.

Soon after his wins in the Chevrolet TC coupe and the Volpi-Chevrolet Fangio was part of the group sent to the USA and Europe in May on a reconnaissance mission by the ACA. He travelled with Oscar Galvez and Pascal Puopolo, Juan Carlos Gozzi from the Automobile Club and Ricardo Nasi a director of the national petroleum company YPF. Among

Christian Huet:
"a certain collusion with Gordini"

Christian Huet, scale model maker, historic car expert, motorcar and racing historian met Fangio on several occasions. He was a close friend of Amédée Gordini about whom he wrote a 'magnum opus' "Amédée Gordini, The Sorcerer and his Team." Here he recalls how the two men met and the friendship that blossomed between them. "Before the Temporada Amédée Gordini had never seen Fangio race. As you know the Argentinean government paid for the transport of two cars, one of which had to be entrusted to a local driver. Fangio was chosen by Gordini because of his piercing look! They met up frequently after that. Whenever Amédée called Fangio he came without hesitation and was always available. He drove for Gordini again in 1950 in the Le Mans 24 Hours with Gonzalez in the 1500 cc car, in Paris in 1951 and in Bordeaux in an F2 single-seater in 1953. Then at the start of 1956 he tested the streamlined 8 cylinder F1 at Montlhéry when it was presented to the press. He did that to help Gordini find money. He was a loyal friend and used to come to the mechanics' dinner at Gordini's on the Boulevard Victor in Paris every year. He was a close mate of Robert Aumaître's, the Gordini chief mechanic. Fangio had very good memories of Amédée and his last cars including the frog-eyed 4 cylinder car. Up to 1978 Juan Manuel kept a close eye on his work. He spoke to me about it after Gordini's death. The fact that they both had parents of Italian origin certainly helped to cement the ties between them."

• **15**_Christian Huet presents his book "Gordini, the Sorcerer and his Team" on 2nd October 1984 in the presence of Juan Manuel Fangio and Patrick Tambay. In front of them is one of the 1500 cc turbocharged V6 F1 engines.
(Renault Press – Christian Moity archives)

their tasks was the assessment of the level of competition and equipment as well as making contact with the constructors: they also had to give the ACA information about the best racing cars available with a view to a more ambitious programme for the 1949 season. They passed through Detroit visiting the big car factories and then attended the Indianapolis 500 Miles race won by Mauri Rose in a Dedit chassis powered by an Offenhauser engine after an epic struggle with Duke Nalon's Roadster. Fangio was completely bewitched by the race and promised himself that he would drive in it one day. It was one of the few dreams he did not fulfil.

Naturally enough their visit to Europe began in Italy where they made contact with Alfa Romeo in Milan and then Maserati and Ferrari in Modena. On 27th June they attended the San Remo Grand Prix in which their fellow countryman, Clemar Bucci, was racing as was Achille Varzi who gave them advice and renewed his support. The following week found them in Berne for the Swiss and European Grand Prix in Bremgarten. During practice Varzi in his 158 Alfa Romeo went off at low speed for unexplained

reasons. The car overturned killing the unfortunate Italian instantly, an accident that was to have long-term ramifications for Fangio's career. A few days later the Argentinean delegation was at Galiate near Novare to pay a final tribute to a driver who, with Nuvolari, Rosemeyer and Caracciola, was one of the greats of the thirties, the "Era of the Titans" which exercises a strong fascination even today. In painful circumstances Fangio and his friends met Achille's father the engineer Menotti Varzi who became a friend.

The Berne circuit was one of the most dangerous in Europe because of a 7.280 km layout that combined tarmac and cobble stones and twisted its way through a tree-lined park which led to constant changes in visibility, light and grip between the wet and dry sections due to the irregular but frequent showers of the Swiss German summer. The 1948 event was a particularly deadly one. The Italian rider, Omobono Tenni, was killed during the Motor Cycle Grand Prix, and then local lad Christian Kautz crashed in front of his public in his Maserati killing himself instantly.

• **16**_18ᵗʰ July 1948: Juan
Manuel Fangio's Grand Prix
debut at the wheel of a Simca-
Gordini in the A.C.F Grand
Prix. He retired due to
mechanical problems.
*(Photo Christian Moity - DR
archives)*

Another accident, fortunately without fatal
consequences, happened during the supporting
race for small capacity cars prior to the Grand
Prix. Frenchman, Maurice Trintignant, went off
and was thrown out of his Simca-Gordini (in that
era European single-seaters had neither roll bars
nor seat belts). By some miracle Robert Manzon,
who was close behind, managed to avoid his
compatriot lying on the track. Help arrived almost
immediately and the popular "Petoulet" suffering
from a punctured spleen and multiple fractures
including his skull, was rushed to hospital in a
critical condition. His heart stopped beating for a
few seconds but miraculously and against all
expectations he survived to race again. He was,
however, laid up for many months' convalescence.
Amédée Gordini was looking for a driver to
replace him for the small car race and the A.C.F
Grand Prix on the Reims-Gueux circuit on
18ᵗʰ July, and knowing that Fangio was in Italy
and available Gordini sent him a telegramme
asking him to drive for his team in these two
events. Juan Manuel accepted straight away even
though he knew that the little Simca-Gordinis
were neither quick nor reliable enough for the
billiard-smooth Reims track. While he was in with
a chance in the race for small cubic capacity cars
he knew that the Gordini was far too slow to
challenge the powerful Alfettas, the quick 4 CLT
Maseratis plus the lumbering 4.5 litre Lago Talbots
in the main race. It would be experience he said
to himself and enable him to rub shoulders with
the cream of Grand Prix drivers.

And it all turned out as expected. In the
small capacity race he was second quickest in
practice and was fighting with Raymond Sommer,
the winner, for the lead when he had to retire
due to a punctured fuel tank. In the Grand Prix
itself won by Wimille in his Alfa Romeo he
managed to stay in the slipstream of the more
powerful cars until the engine blew after 41 laps.
So the meeting ended in two retirements. ∎

Chapter 6
1949
The rising of a champion

Fangio's international career really took off in 1949. Heeding his advice and that of the other members of the exploratory mission the ACA bought a pair of new 4 CLT Maseratis plus two Simca-Gordinis. They were entrusted to Juan Manuel and Benedicto Campos, who seemed to have the makings of a good driver, after Oscar Galvez decided he did not want a career abroad.

On 29th January the 1949 Temporada began in Buenos Aires. Both 4 CLT Maseratis painted in Argentinean colours (dark blue chassis and yellow bonnet) were entered for Fangio and Andrea Malusardi. Campos had an older model that had belonged to Villoresi who, like his friend, Alberto Ascari, was behind the wheel of a works Maserati. Prince Bira entered his own car as did the British driver Reg Parnell and Nino Farina turned up in a 2 litre supercharged Ferrari.

In practice on Saturday tragedy struck. Jean-Pierre Wimille crashed his Simca-Gordini when he swerved trying to avoid spectators massed too close to the side of the track. The unfortunate driver was seriously injured and died on his admission to the Buenos Aires hospital. The French contingent was deeply upset, as were all the other drivers who had enormous respect for Wimille and none more so than Fangio as he knew what he owed the Frenchman.

He held second place for a long time in the race until a rear tyre exploded on his Maserati. He had both rear wheels replaced in the pits but they were the wrong size and fitted with smaller diameter tyres. Despite this handicap he still finished fourth.

On 6th February in the "Premio Jean-Pierre Wimille" in Palermo Park and on 20th March in Cordoba he won his last two races in "Mecanica Nacional" at the wheel of his Volpi-Chevrolet. Between these he scored his first success in the 4 CLT Maserati on 27th February on the El Torreon circuit in Mar Del Plata, the final race of the Temporada series which was overshadowed by Malusardi's fatal accident in practice. Fangio led from start to finish and soon afterwards he set off for Europe with Benedicto Campos.

Amadeo Bignami, Varzi's former secretary and chief mechanic, was the man who looked after the preparation of the Equipo Argentino's first season in Europe. Following the Italian's fatal accident in Berne the previous year his father, Menotti Varzi, decided to give the equipment and workshop in Galiate between Milan and Turin to the Argentineans. Bignami was taken on by the ACA not only to look after the cars but also show Fangio and Campos the ropes around the European circuits, deal with their entries etc., in

short to act as team manager. Between races they stayed in the house in Galiate lent to them by Varzi. As a mark of respect the team was renamed "Equipo Achille Varzi."

France was the first country to restart racing after the war with an event in the Bois de Boulogne in September 1945, soon followed by Italy. There was plenty of motor racing in these two countries. In a Europe emerging from the horrors and deprivation of the war years there was a huge audience for any form of

● **17**_10ᵗʰ July 1949: the Albi Grand Prix on the Planques circuit which Fangio won in a canter in his 4 CLT/48 Maserati.
(Photo Christian Moity – DR archives)

entertainment or distraction and this included
car or bike racing. They attended events
organised on circuits laid out in parks with tarred
roads, in the centre or on the outskirts of towns
especially by the seaside or lakes. The following is
a non-exhaustive list which in France included
Aix-les-Bains, Albi, Bordeaux, Caen, Marseille,
Nice, Pau, Perpignan, les Sables d'Olonne and in
Italy Bari, Lake Garda, Naples, San Remo, Syracuse
in Sicily and Turin. They were soon imitated by
Belgium (Grand Prix des Frontières in Chimay)
and Switzerland (Montreux and Geneva's "Grand
Prix des Nations"). Of course all forms of racing
were banned in Switzerland in the wake of the
1955 Le Mans disaster. The creation of the F1
World Championship in 1950 did not sound the
death knell of these grands prix, which were run
for F1, F2 and F. Libre cars and attracted entries
from the best teams and drivers of the era.

On 3rd April 1949 the Argentineans and
their Italian team manager arrived in San Remo
to race in the Grand Prix. The 3.3 km Ospedaletti
circuit was a bit like Monaco and Pau. It snaked
its way between the sea and huge clusters of
flowers and included a majority of hairpins and
tight corners requiring precision rather than

outright speed. Fangio and Campos did not hold
out much hope of victory as they were up
against stiff opposition from Bira, Sommer,
Chiron, Rosier etc. In practice Juan Manuel set
pole and then a conrod went. He repaired the
engine himself which his mechanics installed
while he slept.

The next day he scored an easy win in the
first heat after Sommer retired his Ferrari while
into second came Bira, quite a long way behind.
He also won the second doing just what was
necessary to fend off the attacks of the Siamese
driver as the results were decided by the addition
of times. This was an early demonstration of his
legendary race craft.

Fifteen days later he did exactly the same
thing on the Pau circuit on Easter Monday. The
layout was much the same as San Remo, tight,
twisty and hard on brakes, gearboxes, clutches
and engines due to the constantly changing
revs. Again he set pole and won easily from
De Graffenried with Campos coming home third.
On 8th May in the "Grand Prix du Roussillon" on
the Perpignan circuit he repeated his
San Remo success winning both heats and
the race from Bira.

As the season continued he looked increasingly unbeatable and on 22nd May he scored an easy victory in the Marseilles Grand Prix on a circuit laid out in the alleys of the Parc Borély with a section running along the sea front. It must have reminded him of the Mar Del Plata track and this time the 2 Argentineans chose the agile Simca-Gordinis. A violent wind caused the drivers a lot of trouble and at the last moment Bignami fitted a Plexiglas windscreen to Fangio's car which helped him to triumph in the race.

After four wins in four races Juan Manuel was becoming a motor racing idol as famous in France as in Italy and above all in Argentina where the Sojit brothers, two reporters whose volubility was exceeded only by their chauvinism, related their team's exploits on Radio Belgrano, especially Fangio's. It soon became obvious that Campos was not in the same league as his fellow-countryman due to his overall lack of success and his inability to back up his team leader.

On 2nd June his string of successes came to an end in the Rome Grand Prix on the Cracalla circuit. He was advised (wrongly) to drive a Maserati sports car whose engine went during the race. This retirement was a blow to the team, as it needed money to continue. When Fangio arrived in Italy he had made a deal with the director of the Lubra oil company. In exchange for carrying the company's brand on the cars' bodywork he was promised 150 000 lira per victory. After several visits to the Lubra company he managed to get the 600 000 lira owed to the team.

After each win a raft of congratulatory telegrams including official ones arrived from Argentina but it was not enough. The team did not have the money to buy new engines so everybody including Fangio rolled up their sleeves and got their hands dirty. They prepared the two 4 CLTs as best they could in the Galliate workshop for the Belgian Grand Prix on 19th June on the Spa-Francorchamps circuit. Eleven months after Reims it would be Juan Manuel's second "grande épreuve" not long before the launch of the World Championship for Drivers.

The 14.120 km Spa-Francorchamps track wended its way through the Ardennes forest on public roads. It was a magnificent natural circuit made up of several straights and some blindingly fast corners like the Masta esses plus heart-stopping downhill slopes such as the the one in front of the stands before the uphill climb of Eau Rouge which, taken at racing speeds, felt like hitting a wall. Together with the mythic Nürburgring in Germany it was one of the most difficult circuits in the world for both cars and drivers and one of the best for spectators.

Fangio, like all the other great drivers, would have his moments of glory on the Belgian circuit but not this year as the very tired 4 CLT Maseratis of the Achille Varzi. Team were incapable of battling for victory. Ferrari entered a brace of 1.5 litre 12 cylinder supercharged Ferraris for Ascari and Villoresi backed up by English privateer Peter Whitehead. Further opposition to the Argentineans came from Maseratis driven by

● **19**_26th June 1949. Fangio refuelling the F2 166 Ferrari, which the Argentinean team managed to prise out of the Maranello factory with much difficulty. In it he won the all-important Monza Autodromo Grand Prix.
(Photo Auto Italian – Christian Moity archives)

● **20**_Bignami, chief
mechanic of the late Achille
Varzi's team, adjusts Fangio's
Maserati's engine.
*(Photo Christian Moity –
DR archives)*

Farina, Parnell and Ashmore. Also entered was a
host of 4.5 litre French Talbots in the hands of
Etancelin, Rosier, Levegh and Mairesse plus one
for Belgian Johnny Claes. Fangio was on the front
row between Villoresi and Etancelin but he did
not get very far as his engine went at the end of
the first lap (blown piston). Campos, who started
from row 3, also retired due to mechanical
problems. Although the outcome was foreseeable
the team was on the rocks financially and only
took part to get the starting money.

It looked like the Argentineans would have
to throw in the towel before the end of the
season: or at least this is what Fangio announced
on the Sojit brothers' radio. Almost immediately
afterwards he received a promise of financial help
from Argentina. A rich industrialist and Peron
supporter sent money and Maranello received an
emergency order for two F2 Ferrari 166s which
would bring the team victories in the future. In
fact, Francisco Borgonovo, the ACA official, who
was in permanent contact with Fangio, had taken
the risk of ordering new cars from Ferrari before
being sure that he could lay his hands on the
cash! At Ferrari the total production for 1949, just
2 years after the creation of the make, was

21 cars so placing an order was a difficult task
especially as the 166 Barchettas had won two of
the most famous Italian races the Targa Florio on
20th March and the Mille Miglia on 24th April so
orders were flooding in. In addition the first post-
war Le Mans 24 Hour race was coming up and
Ferrari had entered 2 cars for the event.

By chance Borgonovo and the ACA
President Carlos Anesi were in Europe at the same
time for the annual FIA conference. In Milan they
met up with Fangio who assured them that he
had had confirmation by telephone from a friend
close to the Argentinean government of the
imminent arrival of the necessary funds, some
11 000 dollars. All three went to Maranello where
two F2 166 single-seaters were nearing
completion one primed and the other painted in
Italian red. Enzo Ferrari made it quite clear,
however, that they would not be painted in the
Achille Varzi team colours and delivered until the
money had been paid. However, he let Fangio test
one of the cars on the Modena circuit on the
Thursday before the "Grand Prix de l'Autodromo"
scheduled for Sunday 26th June at Monza. Fangio
went out in the Ferrari and immediately realised
that 5th gear did not work.

Enzo Ferrari:
A superior vision of racing

"He had a superior vision of racing, an equilibrium, a competitive intelligence and a confidence in negotiating the race that were quite unusual. I remember the incident, which I would consider the most significant, even if it may not be the most sensational of his career. In June 1949 he was driving in the Monza Grand Prix on the Autodromo, rebuilt by Luigi Bertett, in a Ferrari that I'd given to the Argentinean team. He went straight into the lead followed by the Ferraris of Ascari, Villoresi, Bonetto and Cortese. Lap after lap he inched out a small lead but towards the end of the race he slowed and his pursuers began to catch him. What was happening? Bignami, who had been Nuvolari's and then Varzi's mechanic, was now with Fangio and he started to panic without knowing what was going on, and picking up a wheel and a lead hammer got ready to signal Fangio to come in for a bogus refuelling stop. The late Bignami preferred seeing his hero beaten for reasons of force majeure rather then being caught and passed after dominating the race. I was in the pits at that very moment as it was the epoch when I still attended grands prix. But something that had not escaped me was the way Fangio stared fixedly at the dashboard each time he passed the pits. I guessed what was wrong. The oil temperature was rising dangerously. Fangio was afraid of the engine blowing up before the finish and he slowed to keep it at a reasonable temperature so I intervened to stop Bignami carrying out his plan. There was a moment of uncertainty. Then with just one lap to go Fangio upped his pace and won the race. Bignami looked at me, smiled and rushed to his driver who finished his lap of honour with his arms raised in the air in a gesture of sheer joy. A short time afterwards the Argentinean confirmed that the oil temperature had indeed gone up."
(Enzo Ferrari: Piloti, che Gente)

After official practice at Monza the car was delivered to the paddock while the works cars of Ascari and Villoresi and Bonetto's private entry were still lapping the circuit. It was not until Borgonovo and Anesi had signed an acknowledgement of debt that Ferrari let Fangio take possession of the car at the very last moment. Fifth gear was still unusable. The Ferrari mechanics had not been able (or did not want to) repair the gearbox. The Argentinean was thus obliged to race on this very fast circuit with long straights with only 4 speeds. Luckily they were long ratios as he said later.

The "Grand Prix de l'Autodromo" was held in front of a large crowd at the very moment when several hundred kilometres away, Chinetti was about to give Ferrari his first Le Mans 24 Hours victory. As forecast the race was a no-holds-barred battle between the works Ferraris and the Argentinean private entry (still painted red). Towards half-distance Fangio realised that when he was hitting the revs ceiling at 7200 rpm in 4th, 500 over the limit recommended by the constructor, his engine overheated and lost oil. Luckily for him Ascari and Villoresi had both had problems and lost time in the pits. Once again

● **21**_17th July 1949: Fangio and his F2 166 Ferrari before the start of the small capacity cup on the Reims circuit. He retired due to mechanical problems.
(Photo Christian Moity – DR archives)

Fangio managed to nurse his engine to the finish and won the Grand Prix from Bonetto and Ascari. Ferrari scored a triple but not in the order that the Commendatore wanted! After the race Ferrari sent the Achille Varzi team a bill for 300 000 lira for repairs without acknowledging that the factory was at fault or that Fangio's amazing feat was excellent publicity for the fledgling make! Several years later, though, Enzo Ferrari did pay homage to Juan Manuel for his drive that day.

Finally, the long-awaited money from Argentina arrived and the team was able to settle its debt to Ferrari. Fangio's car was repaired and painted blue and yellow in time for the race on the Reims circuit. In the meantime both 4 CLT Maseratis had been rebuilt at the factory in Modena either with the 600 000 lira from Lubra or the prize money from the Monza victory. They were brought to Albi where there was a Grand Prix on 10th July on the Planques circuit at the gates of the historic town. Fangio and Campos found themselves up against their friend and rival Prince Bira. He ran into an engine problem in practice and Fangio listening to his heart (and

not Bignami who was against) lent him his only spare engine. It was a magnanimous gesture. The following day the Argentinean beat Bira who again finished second.

Fangio had won six out of seven races and even if some of them were minor events his Monza victory was of considerable importance. Would he be able to do as well at Reims on 17th July, the circuit on which he had made his European debut? No was the answer. In the small capacity cup run to F2 regulations and renamed the "Jean-Pierre Wimille Cup" in homage to the great French driver, he was driving a Ferrari and battling with the front-runners until his gear lever broke, victory going to Ascari. In the Formula 1 event, the French Grand Prix* Fangio and Campos were back in their Maseratis. Both Argentineans were on form and swapped the lead in the race. Campos was in attack mode that day as he led everybody including Juan Manuel for several laps. The latter went out on lap 25 with a broken clutch while Campos, who was still in the lead at half-distance, retired with a blown valve.

Despite his retirement at Reims Fangio confirmed that he had nothing to envy the best Grand Prix drivers of the era and was able to match the pace of Ascari, Villoresi, Farina, Bira, Rosier, Sommer or veteran Louis Chiron who won the race in his Lago-Talbot. He did not race in any other events after the French Grand Prix but did not arrive home in Argentina until 25th August. This was because he took a well-deserved holiday with his girlfriend Dona Andreina known as "Beba" and also made a few useful contacts.

A cheering crowd greeted him at the Buenos Aires airport as a national hero and he took all the acclaim in his usual modest stride. Perhaps what gave him the most pleasure was a banner on which was written "the Galvistas salute Fangio" which effectively buried an old rivalry. He was then congratulated personally by President Peron at a reception in the presidential palace after which Suixtil laid on a gala dinner for him.

Finally he was able to escape from the capital and headed home to Balcarce. There at the entry to the town he was again acclaimed by an enthusiastic crowd followed by a joyful reunion with his parents and brothers and sisters.

The year was not over yet and Fangio thrilled his home crowd when he got behind the wheel of a Chevrolet coupe in the "Gran Premio de la Republica de Carreteras" held between 5th and 27th November. He saw the chequered flag in 2nd place splitting the Galvez brothers with victory going to Juan, the younger while Oscar finished third. Juan Manuel said that he had lost the knack of driving a "Turismo de Carreteras" and that the Galvez brothers were now the top dogs in this form of racing. It was to be his last appearance in such an event. On 18th December just before the start of summer in the southern hemisphere he finished second in a 125 1500 cc supercharged Ferrari in the "Premio J.-D. Peron" on the Palermo Park circuit. ■

*That year the ACF Grand Prix was a sports car event held on 7th August on the Saint-Guadens circuit. It was won by Charles Pozzi (Delahaye) who would later become the Ferrari importer for France.

● **23**_26th August 1949: Juan Manuel Fangio's triumphal return to Buenos Aires. He was given a warm welcome by President General Peron (on the right), M. Aloé the mayor of the Argentinean capital; and on the left Eva Peron, the president's wife.
(Photo Christian Moity - DR archives)

Chapter 7
1950
Fame with
Alfa Romeo

When Fangio came back to Argentina he told his friends that he had received a very tempting offer from Alfa Romeo to drive for the factory in the 1950 F1 Grands Prix. The Milan company whose racing cars bore the famous "Quadrifologio Verde" symbol following the legendary P2's victory in the 1924 Constructors World Championship, won all the Grands Prix in which they raced in 1947 and 48. The 158 Alfetta was now part of motor racing legend and was one of the most beautiful single-seaters ever built. It was designed by the engineer, Giaocchino Colombo, in 1937 and developed in Enzo Ferrari's workshops in Modena. Initially it was destined for the "Voiturette" category, the Formula 2 or F3000 equivalent of the day. In 1947, the new F1 rules drawn up by the FIA stated that an unsupercharged car could have a maximum cubic capacity of 4.5 litres and a supercharged one 1500 ccs. The 1500 cc 8 cylinder supercharged Alfetta was among the cars complying with this formula. Its straight eight engine with single stage supercharging initially put out 225 bhp and its power output was gradually increased to fend off its rivals particularly after the creation of the world championship in 1950. In 1948, the two stage supercharged engine was giving 350 bhp and Alfa Romeo wiped the board thanks to a top-class team of drivers led by Jean-Pierre Wimille (who would have been world champion had the title existed) backed up by veteran Achille Varzi, Count Felice Trossi and test driver Consalvo Sanesi. Varzi's fatal accident in Berne in July 1948 followed by Wimille's in January 1949 and Trossi's death on 9th May of the same year due to cancer had decimated the team just at the time when Ferrari was becoming a force to be reckoned with and the 4 CLT Maseratis were reaching the peak of their development. So Alfa Romeo gave the 1949 season a miss.

Alfa Romeo's official return was due to the fact that it could not remain absent from Grand Prix racing much longer especially as a world championship had been created. Certainly it was a Drivers' Championship (the Constructors' title did not come into existence until 1958) but victory in it could not fail to embellish the reputation of the make. There was also another reason driven by commercial necessity: the launch of the Alfa Romeo 1900 which in coupe, saloon or cabriolet form marked the firm's first venture into the realm of series production vehicles.

Initially, Fangio considered doing the 1950 Grand Prix season as an independent in either a Ferrari or the new V12 Osca. The latter was not ready and Ferrari did not want to sell one of his cars to the Argentinean knowing that he would either win races or finish in the top three thus depriving the Maranello piggy bank of large amounts of starting money.*

This was the context in which Alfa Romeo approached Fangio as the company's president, Antonio Alessi, and competitions manager, Battista Guidotti, had both seen his dominant win in San Remo. And so the new team - which became known as the three FA's - was born: it consisted of two Italian Grand Prix stars of the 30s Luigi Fagioli and Nino Farina, both known for their fiery temperament despite their years of experience especially Farina whose hard driving tactics had already had fatal consequences. Fangio, the third FA, hesitated before accepting. First of all as he was the only non-Italian in the team he was the centre of the kind of chauvinistic storm in a teacup typical of the nationalistic press. 'Was there not another Italian driver good enough to be included in the team', screamed the journalists? The answer was no as Ascari, Villoresi and Taruffi were all under contract to Ferrari. Another hurdle in the early negotiations was an exclusivity clause in the contract but Fangio was adamant about keeping his options open for events not counting for the world championship. Finally, the following solution was found: Alfa Romeo gave him freedom of choice to race in events in which the Milan company was not competing. And so he signed. In 1949, he had left home to do a season's racing in Europe after which he intended to return to Balcarce and take up his job of garage owner and lorry dealer, but once he had tasted the joys of Grand Prix racing he decided that his future lay in becoming a professional racing driver.

In January Fangio took part in the Temporada Series. His three races with the 166 Ferrari yielded mediocre results (a fourth place in Buenos Aires and a couple of retirements in Mar Del Plata and Rosario). Then it was time for him to come back to Europe and in March he had his first close look at the Alfetta 158 in Milan. He was not unfamiliar with the car, as he had seen Wimille win the French Grand Prix in 1948 in an Alfa. In the meantime it had evolved even further in both power and driveability and Juan Manuel got in behind the wheel of one of the cars whose cover had been removed.

He was over the moon and declared "this car fits me like a glove!" While awaiting the first private test sessions his confidence was boosted by the working ambience in the team managed by Guidotti, Nuvolari's pre-war team-mate and mechanic. Many years after his retirement Fangio said that Alfa Corse was the most professional team he had worked with after Mercedes-Benz.

His first race was the Marseille Grand Prix on 19th March in which he finished third in a Ferrari 125. Then came his debut for Alfa Romeo before the opening round of the world championship, the San Remo Grand Prix on 16th April. In addition, his was the only Alfa Romeo entered for a race in which he had scored his maiden European victory the previous year, as Farina had had an accident a short time before. He was quickest in practice and made a cautious start on the wet track learning to dose the 158's phenomenal acceleration. He revealed later that during the first two or three laps he was extremely ill at ease because his contract with the Milan firm had not yet been signed, and if he crashed the beautiful Alfa his detractors would shoot him down. He soon came to terms with the delicate touch required by the car, overtook his rivals one by one, and won the Grand Prix hands down from Villoresi's Ferrari. This shut his critics up although he still had to prove himself in the world championship. For Alessio, though, he'd shown that he was made of the right stuff and he gave the Argentinean the contract to sign in the San Remo hotel on the evening of the race. Money had always been Fangio's smallest worry.

• **28**_21st May 1950: Fangio
on his way to his first F1 World
Championship victory in
Monaco passes the wreckage of
the cars involved in a first lap
pile up in the Bureau de Tabac
corner. His foresight enabled
him to avoid the crash.
*(Centro di Documentazione
Storice Alfa Romeo – William
Huon archives)*

Now that a prestigious company was paying him
to race whereas in the past he had always had to
fork out money for his drives he said to Alessio,
"just add the number of zeros that suits you !"

While awaiting the start of the F1 World
Championship, the British and European Grand
Prix on the Silverstone circuit on 13th May, the
new Alfa Romeo driver, polyvalent like all drivers
until the 70s, was down to drive a sports 6 C
2500 coupe in a road event that he was
competing in for the first time, the Mille Miglia
on 23rd April. It was a crazy race run on open
roads in Italy starting and finishing in Brescia in a
mind-boggling festive atmosphere. It consisted of
a single 1 600 km leg covered once. It was full of
traps and dangers like changes in the road
surface, grip, poor visibility, level crossings, hump-
backed bridges and passes crossed in fog added to
which were the massed ranks of frenzied
spectators on either side of the road. Despite the

vigilance of the Carabinieri it was not uncommon
for the more reckless among them to dash across
the road just as a car was approaching at high
speed.

It was a kind of mixture of the "Giro
d'Italia" cycle race, which used part of the same
route and appealed to the same spectators who
cheered on their heroes like Fausto Coppi, and a
special stage in a rally. The only stops allowed
were for refuelling and tyre changes at the
service points which the works teams set up just
beside the official check points to waste as little
time as possible. There was neither neutralization
nor parc fermé and the crews had their cards
stamped and car refuelled (sometimes themselves
too) in quick succession. The start was given at
one minute intervals to more than 600 cars come
to tackle this road marathon in which were
entered works cars and drivers but also privateers,
garage owners, tuners like Abarth or Nardi, simple

tinkerers or gentlemen drivers (including cinema stars like Roberto Rossellini) there to generate publicity for themselves or just to get their yearly dose of adrenalin.

The Mille Miglia was organised for the first time in 1927 and survived until 1957. Fangio raced in it five times. His partner on his first outing in the race was an Alfa Romeo mechanic, Zanardi, imposed by Alessio. Since Urrutia's death he was not very happy about the idea of having a passenger on board as it was obligatory according to the regulations until 1953; from 1954, several drove the event single-handed. Alessio convinced him that it would be a good idea in case of trouble and in addition, the mechanic knew the route like the back of his hand a big help for Fangio who had had no time to carry out reconnaissance. He and Zanardi worked out a form of sign language and the latter tapped his hand on the dashboard once,

twice or three times depending on the degree of danger of the corner. At the start he told Fangio not to exceed 5000 rpm. When they were passed by Bonetto, a Mille Miglia regular, in a 4.5 litre Alfa Romeo after refuelling in Pescara, Zanardi shouted to Fangio, "5500 rpm." The Argentinean obeyed and helped over the Pennines towards the end of the race by Franco Cortese, another regular, whose traces he followed he reached Brescia without problems. He finished 3rd overall behind the Marzotto-Crosara and Serafini-Salani Ferrari 212 Inters: not bad for a first attempt!

After the Mille Miglia it was decided that Zanardi would become chief mechanic on Fangio's Alfetta. In compliance with his contract Juan Manuel raced in the Modena Grand Prix in a Ferrari and then rejoined the Alfa Corse squad for practice for the British Grand Prix on the Silverstone circuit, a disused RAF aerodrome on

● **29**_Fangio wins the Monaco Grand Prix, the first of his 24 F1 World Championship victories. History is in the making.
(Autocar – Quadrant Picture Library)

P. MÉNARD

Designer: Gioacchino Colombo

Engine
Make/type: Alfa Romeo 158
Number of cylinders/configuration: Straight 8 (FR)
Cubic Capacity: 1479 ccs
Bore/stroke: 58 x 70 mm
Compression ratio: 6.5:1
Superchargers: 2 (Roots)
Max. power: 350 bhp
Max. Revs: 8500 rpm
Block: light alloy
Carburation: Triple barrel
Distribution: D.O.H.C
No. of valves per cylinder: 2
Ignition: 2 magnetos (Marelli)

Transmission
Gearbox, No. of speeds: Alfa Romeo longitudinal (4)
Clutch: Alfa Romeo

Chassis
Type: Twin tube ladder frames
Suspension: Independent, raked wheels, transverse leaf spring
(Front) : independent pivot links and de Dion axle (Rear)
Dampers: telescopic friction.
Wheels: 600.18 – 550.17 (front) 700.18 (Rear)
Tyres: Pirelli
Brakes: Alfa Romeo drums mounted in the wheels

Dimensions
Wheelbase: 2500 mm
Tracks: 1250 mm (front and rear)
Dry Weight: 700 kgs
Fuel tanks' capacity: 185 litres

Raced from Great Britain to Italy.

which the BRDC (British Racing Drivers Club) had laid out a 4.548 km circuit. It was a medium speed track much different from the one used today and the fastest lap in practice was just over 150 km/h. There were no Ferraris at the start as the Scuderia preferred to send its cars and drivers to a minor race in Belgium, which promised loads of starting money. Alfa Romeo entered four 158s, the usual three for the 3 FAs plus an entry for Brit Reg Parnell. Among the opposition the main threat to the Alfas appeared to come from the four 4 CLT Maseratis in particular those entered by the Ecurie Platé for Bira and De Graffenried and Louis Chiron's factory backed car. Also present were five Lago-Talbots including those driven by Frenchmen Etancelin and Rosier and the rest of the grid consisted of five British cars, three ERAs and two Altas, which had no chance of victory.

All the drivers were presented to King George VI and the Royal family on an official visit to Silverstone to mark the occasion, Fangio, though, did not have very happy memories of the first F1 World Championship Grand Prix. It was a rather boring walkover for the Alfa Romeos and their drivers; and for the spectators it was not all that exciting either as the majority of Maseratis and Talbots hit mechanical problems. For most of the race the Argentinean was sandwiched between Fagioli and Farina, who set the lap record at 151.314 km/h, until lap 62 of the seventy scheduled for the race, when his oil pressure went through the floor. Farina headed an Alfa triple followed by Fagioli and Parnell.

A week later Fangio got a well-deserved revenge in only his second Grand Prix for Alfa Romeo in conditions that again showed his race craft and prudence as well as his brio. Enzo Ferrari

would have to stop twice. He almost won his bet as at half-distance after the Alfa Romeos had stopped once he was in the lead. Ascari in the Ferrari 275 was slowed by repeated wheel changes. Fangio and Farina were once again locked in battle for the lead passing and repassing each other. They both overtook Sommer who was still in with a shout, as the 158s would have to stop again for fuel. Alas, the Talbot's 6-cylinder engine expired soon afterwards and Fangio went on to win with 19 seconds in hand over Fagioli. Farina who set the lap record, came home 4th behind Rosier's Talbot which, in hindsight, showed that Sommer's strategy was the right one.

Then came the ACF Grand Prix on the Reims Gueux circuit on 2nd July where Fangio scored a clean sweep: pole position, victory and fastest lap (over 180 km/h). There were no works Ferraris as the Scuderia was concentrating on sorting out its new unsupercharged cars so it was another fairly

processional Grand Prix as the Lago Talbots and Maseratis stopped one after the other with overheated engines or blown pistons. The scorching heat that day was very hard on both men and machines. Farina was forced to stop twice due to his fuel feed system going on the blink. The first time was at his pit and his mechanics resolved the problem. Nino went back out in eighth place and began to carve his way up through the field until the same thing reoccurred in the Thillois corner. He got out and courageously pushed his Alfa Romeo across the finishing line in the sweltering conditions to finish seventh. Fangio went on to victory as Fagioli - the eternal second - was 25.7s behind at the finish. Farina had not scored in the world championship so Fangio now led with 25 points, one more than his two Italian team-mates. The last event of the season, the Italian Grand Prix, promised a breath-taking finale to decide the outcome of the championship.

● **34**_Another double for the Alfettas with Fangio and Fagioli again finishing in that order in the ACF Grand Prix. A sporting Nino Farina joins in the celebration despite his disappointment. Or maybe he just likes champagne!
(Centro di Documentazione Storice Alfa Romeo – William Huon archives)

Angoulême:
a very tough race

On the "Circuit des Remparts" in Angoulème a very twisty track laid out in the city Fangio tested his legendary endurance to the limit on 11th June winning a long and exhausting Formula Libre race in a 4 CLT Maserati powered by a 2 litre 6-cylinder F2 engine running on alcohol. In 1987, he came back to Angoulème for the "Grand Prix Retrospective" on the "Circuit des Remparts" and told us the story of his 1950 win. "The race was 130 laps. It was very hot and the gearbox was not much good. I screwed up the start and I really had to push to catch the field and overtake my rivals. When finally I was in the lead I was finished and I thought the race was nearly over. Then I received a signal telling me there were 100 laps left! I'd only done 20. Luckily, a spectator took pity on me and threw a bucket of water over me to help me keep going. It was one hell of a tough race!"

Weekends and races followed one another in quick succession, each one different. Between the Belgian Grand Prix and that of the ACF came the Le Mans 24 Hours race organised by the A.C.O. Fangio agreed to drive in it in a pretty little coupe (T 15 C no.33) to help his friend Amédée Gordini. It was the first of his four appearances in the Sarthe. His co-driver was Gonzalez now fully recovered from his Monaco accident. The Gordini was a 4 cylinder supercharged 1500 cc model: it was light, fast but reliability was not its strong point. Trintignant and Manzon shared an identical car in which they managed to get up to sixth overall before retiring with a water leak. The two Argentineans were in ninth place when the distribution broke during the thirteenth hour.

On 9ᵗʰ July Alfa Romeo Corse entered for the non-championship Bari Grand Prix and Fangio finished second behind Farina. The highlight of the race was the performance of a young and very promising English driver, Stirling Moss. In his outclassed F2 HWM he hassled the Alfas mercilessly finishing third just behind the red cars.

On the Albi circuit on 16ᵗʰ July and at Zandvoort on the 23ʳᵈ Fangio had his last couple of outings in his old 4 CLT Maserati in two non-championship Grands Prix both of which ended in retirement with mechanical problems. He then won two Grands Prix for Alfa Romeo neither of which counted for the championship. They were the Grand Prix des Nations in Geneva on 30ᵗʰ July his team-mates on this occasion being the Swiss driver Toulo De Graffenried and Piero Taruffi. The 158s scored a triple in the Swiss event and then came the Pescara Grand Prix on 15ᵗʰ August. This circuit on the Adriatic coast had a very long straight that included a special 1 km timed section. A special prize was awarded to the driver setting the highest speed, which Fangio also won. He was timed at 310 km/h, which is pretty impressive when one thinks of the tyres on these cars and the narrowness of the track.

On 26ᵗʰ August Juan Manuel came second in the BRDC International Trophy at Silverstone a week before the championship clincher, the Italian Grand Prix on the Monza circuit on 3ʳᵈ September. Alfa Corse entered no fewer than five cars and backing up the 3 FAs were Piero Taruffi and test driver Consalvo Sanesi. This was not only to put on a show for its home crowd but also to counter the growing threat from Ferrari. The Scuderia entered a couple of its new 4.5 litre unsupercharged 375s designed by Aurelio Lampredi but the team's hopes suffered a setback when Villoresi had an accident prior to the race. His replacement alongside Ascari was Dorino Serafini, better known for his exploits on motorbikes than cars. The remainder of the entry was made up of the usual Maseratis, Lago Talbots and Simca Gordinis plus a strange hybrid, a Jaguar-engined Ferrari for Clemente Biondetti, the Mille Miglia specialist. Twenty-seven cars lined up with Fangio on pole and sharing the front row with him was Ascari, second-fastest, Farina and Sanesi. The battle for the lead raged between Ascari and Farina until lap 22 when the Ferrari's engine blew. Alberto then took over Serafini's car and fought his way back up to second place. Fangio's engine went and Farina cruised home to an easy victory and the first F1 World Championship title. The other contender, Fagioli, saw the flag in third place. The Argentinean's only consolation was 1 point for the fastest lap but it was obvious that he was as quick if not quicker than Farina. The performance of the Ferraris was a foretaste of the 1951 season when Alfa Romeo would not have it all its own way.

When Fangio returned to Argentina as runner-up in the world championship he received another rapturous welcome. He competed in three events, two in his Ferrari 166 on the Entre'Rios circuit and at Palme in Chile which he won. The last was in Sante Fe in Argentina, the Rafaela 500 Miles which he also won at the wheel of a 4.5 litre Lago-Talbot from Frenchman, Louis Rosier.

All in all 1950 had been a very successful season for Fangio. His popularity in Europe had shot up as the spectators had taken the stocky Argentinean with the piercing blue eyes and soft voice, dressed in his yellow short-sleeved shirt and blue linen helmet, to their hearts. The next year would see the mechanic from Balcarce become part of motor racing legend. ∎

* Enzo Ferrari usually shared the prize money with his drivers on a 50/50 basis as at that time they had no basic salary.

● **36**_ Fangio was back in Europe for the second F1 World Championship for Drivers. Here he is seated in his new title challenger, the Type 159 Alfa Romeo.
(Centro di Documentazione Storica Alfa Romeo – Williams Hiton archives)

Chapter 8

1951
Fangio's first World Championship title

Fangio resigned with Alfa Romeo for 1951 but as the World Championship did not begin until the end of May he had time to expand his business activities in Argentina. In addition to his garage in Balcarce he opened a Mercedes-Benz dealership in Buenos Aires, which was the start of a special relationship with the German company. This enabled Daimler Benz to gain a foothold in Argentina and 1951 was also the year when Mercedes made a timid return to the Grand Prix scene. The company sent Alfred Neubauer, the legendary team manager, and a team of mechanics and drivers to race in the Temporada. Out of the museum came a trio of the 1939 W 163 single-seaters powered by a supercharged V12 3-litre engine. Driverwise Neubauer chose two Germans, Hermann Lang and Karl Kling and entrusted the third car to Fangio. Neubauer thought that an easy victory was his for the taking thanks to the power of the Mercedes (around 480 bhp) but in Buenos Aires where the two events took place, the circuit was not the Parc Palermo layout but the very slow and twisty Costanera Norte track. The Mercedes-Benz were handicapped by their weight and the agile

Ferraris proved much better suited to the conditions. In the "Premier Ciudad de Buenos Aires" Fangio could do no better than third and six days later in the "Premio Eva Peron" he retired. Victory in both events went to his friend the tubby Froilan Gonzalez.

Juan Manuel's first race in Europe was at Silverstone where he discovered Colombo's latest evolution of the Alfetta 159 which had a de Dion rear axle, larger fuel tanks and a power output increased to 425 bhp. In theory this was more than enough to match the Ferrari 375's 380 bhp, Alfa's closest rival for world championship honours, as the V16 BRM was still an unknown quantity. The International Trophy on 6th May, run in two heats and a final, was a kind of shakedown for the championship. Fangio won the first Farina the second and the final was stopped after six laps because of torrential rain victory going Reg Parnell in the Thinwall Special Ferrari.

The Argentinean's next two events the Grand Prix de l'Autodromo in a Ferrari and the Paris Grand Prix in a Simca-Gordini both ended in retirement due to mechanical problems. Then came the first round of the world championship,

the Swiss Grand Prix on the Berne circuit, following the cancellation of the Monaco event. Four 159 Alfas were entered for Fangio, Farina, Swiss De Graffenried and Sanesi (Fagioli was absent) and in the three Ferrari 375s were Ascari, Villoresi and Taruffi. Among the other entries was Swiss driver Rudi Fischer in a 2.6 litre Ferrari, Peter Whitehead in his old 125 renamed the Thinwall Special, a couple of 4 CLT Maseratis for Chiron and Schell, two HWMs (Moss and Abecassis) an F2 Veritas (Hirt) and no fewer than seven Lago Talbots one of which was driven by Gonzalez.

Once again Fangio was on pole and shared the front row with Farina and Villoresi ahead of Sanesi and De Graffenried. Ascari, still suffering from burns after an accident in a race in Italy the week before the Swiss event, was on the third row between Taruffi and Rosier's Talbot.

The Grand Prix was run in heavy rain. Farina was the only one of the Alfa Romeo team to start with full tanks (300 litres!) reckoning he could complete the distance without refuelling but Nino got it all wrong. His three team-mates started on half-full tanks with a refuelling stop scheduled

for half-distance. Fangio went straight into the lead from Farina followed by Sanesi, Villoresi, De Graffenried and Ascari. When the Argentinean refuelled Farina went into the lead as he anticipated but not for long. The Argentinean rejoined and driving a perfect race on what had become a skating rink on which the cars' tyres threw up huge clouds of spray, passed Farina a few laps later and pulled away. The world champion made no effort to fight back as he was probably worn out with having to cope with his car's weight since the start. Fangio drove on to victory setting the fastest lap in the process. Into second came Taruffi who overtook an exhausted Farina near the end.

In striking contrast Spa was bathed in sweltering heat for the next round of the championship, the Belgian Grand Prix on 17ᵗʰ June. This time there were only three Alfettas down to race and in practice the cars, running on 17" wheels, were over-revving on the downhill Masta straight and other fast sections of this ultra-rapid circuit. Guidotti solved the problem by having 19" wheels sent from Milan and reducing the engine revs. They did not arrive till Sunday

● **38**_26ᵗʰ May 1951: Fangio and Gonzalez take a break during practice for the Swiss Grand Prix. Initially they were great mates and mutually supportive of each other. Then their rivalry created tension between them which was not resolved until Onofre Marimon's death in the 1954 German Grand Prix at the Nürburgring.

and were fitted to the cars just before the start,
something that was to cost Fangio dear. Again he
dominated practice setting pole in 4m 25s
followed by Farina in 4m 28s and Villoresi in
4m 29s. Battling with Farina for the lead he broke
the lap record tenth time round in 4m 22.1s, a
speed of 193.941 km/h. He was in front when he
came in on lap 15 for a tyre change that went all
wrong. It lasted 14 minutes! Not for a moment
did he display any signs of annoyance, which
impressed all those who witnessed the incident
including Paul Frère (see insert). He charged back

out but despite his efforts he finished in a totally
unmerited 9th place. Farina scored an easy victory
sharing the rostrum with Ascari and Villoresi.

After the Le Mans 24 Hours in which he
partnered his friend Louis Rosier, the 1950 winner,
in a Talbot (they retired in the 9th hour) he came
to Reims for the ACF Grand Prix and put himself
back in contention for the title even though it all
nearly went wrong again. He set his third
consecutive pole in 2m 25.7s ahead of Farina
2m 27.4s and Ascari 2m 28.1s. On the second row
were Villoresi and Sanesi and on the third

Paul Frère:
"His amazing calm"

Belgian Paul Frère, who became a racing driver thanks to his job as journalist and test driver, won the Touring Car Grand Prix held on the Spa circuit the same day as the Grand Prix. He has very vivid memories of Fangio and his Belgian races. "The first time I saw him was at Spa in 1950 and what struck me immediately was that he was much quicker than Farina who wasn't exactly hanging about. Also during practice he was extremely open to the other drivers. He gave advice to anyone who asked for it and contrary to some others, it was right. I remember a Belgian driver who was making his Grand Prix debut asked how he managed to lap so quickly: he answered with a hint of a smile, "more accelerator and less brakes!" And he was right. At Spa in 1951 I was amazed by his extraordinary calm when he stopped at his pit. The mechanics just couldn't remove one of his rear wheels because the hub carrier was jammed. Finally, they were forced to take off the worn tyre and fit a new one on the rim. This took a total of 14 minutes. All Fangio did was to look at his mechanics working and remained completely impassive while Farina, Ascari and Villoresi passed and repassed costing him precious points in the title chase but he said nothing and never showed the slightest signs of irritation."

● **40**_Paul Frère at Le Mans, in 1992.
(Christian Bedeï)

● **41**_During the 1951 Belgian Grand Prix Fangio shows Olympian calm while his mechanics busy themselves trying to remove his Alfa Romeo's wheel. It cost him an almost certain victory.

Gonzalez and Fagioli. In the race Fangio was passed by Ascari and then by Farina who was driving like a bat out of hell. Sanesi's magneto started to play up and he had to have it changed and then Fangio's ignition went on the blink. He stopped on lap 13 for repairs losing a lot of ground. But luckily for him Ascari was in trouble with his brakes and Villoresi's engine was losing power. Breaking the track record on five successive occasions Farina took advantage of his rivals' mishaps to open up a clear lead and Fagioli edged past Villoresi. In that era and up to 1957 the world championship regulations allowed a driver to take over from another during a Grand Prix. Any points scored were then divided between the two men. It was a tactic used frequently by the teams to help the driver who was best placed in the title chase. And so when Fagioli came in to refuel he handed over to Fangio and took over the latter's car, which was

now firing on all eight but way down the field. It was a smart move as the Grand Prix was very long (over 600 kms). Farina was still in front but Juan Manuel was lapping faster than him, set a new lap record and overtook the ailing Villoresi. Gonzalez's refuelling stop let his fellow-countryman into second place. The Ferrari was filled up, rear wheels changed and Froilan handed over to Ascari who got back into second when Fangio came in to refuel. Farina then made a mistake stopping at the pit after his own and had to push his car backwards as allowed by the rules losing three minutes. Ascari should have taken over first place but he had to stop again to have his brakes adjusted. Fangio was now in the lead and stayed there until the finish taking the flag almost one minute ahead of the Ferrari. In the championship it was a good damage-limiting exercise as Farina in fifth scored only two points while Juan Manuel scored five (win shared with

P. MÉNARD

Designer: Gioacchino Colombo

Engine

Make/type: Alfa Romeo 159
Number of cylinders: straight 8 (front)
Cubic capacity: 1479 ccs
Bore/stroke: 58 x 70 mm
Compression ratio: 6.5/1
Superchargers: 2 (Roots)
Max. Power: 425 bhp
Max. Revs: 9300 rpm
Block: light alloy
Carburettors: triple barrel
Distribution: D.O.H.C
Number of valves per cylinder: 2
Ignition: 2 magnetos (Marelli)

Transmission

Gearbox/no. of speeds: Alfa Romeo longitudinal (4)
Clutch: Alfa Romeo

Chassis

Type: Twin tube ladder frame
Suspension: independent, raked wheels, transversal leaf spring
(front) : independent pivot springs, de Dion axle (rear).
Dampers: Telescopic, friction
Wheels: 600.18 – 550.17 (front) 700.18 (rear)
Tyres: Pirelli
Brakes: Alfa Romeo drums mounted in the wheels

Dimensions

Wheelbase: 2500 mm
Tracks: 1250 mm (front and rear)
Dry Weight: 810 kgs
Fuel tanks' capacity: 225 litres

Used from Switzerland to Spain.

Fagioli plus fastest lap) and Ascari and Gonzalez scored three each. Sanesi's Alfa ground to a halt on the last lap and he had to push it several hundred metres under the burning sun to claim tenth spot. The French Grand Prix results showed that Alfa Romeo's superiority was under severe threat from Ferrari and in the battle for the drivers' title the three FAs were faced with strong challenges from Ascari, Gonzalez and Villoresi.

Alfa Romeo met its match in the British Grand Prix on the Silverstone circuit on 14th July. The 1950 event had been a boring procession - and an eminently forgettable debut of the world championship - due in part to the absence of Ferrari. In 1951, however, the spectators were thrilled by an exciting race due to the Scuderia's presence and perhaps even more so by their victory. The teething troubles of the 375s had gradually been sorted out and they were becoming increasingly competitive whereas Alfa

Romeo's power advantage was offset by their excessive thirst. On average they had to stop twice per Grand Prix as against once or not at all for the Ferraris.

However, the focal point of interest for the 100 000 spectators that trooped to Silverstone that day was not the duel between Italians (and Argentineans) but the long-awaited world championship debut of the V16 BRMs driven by Reg Parnell and Peter Walker. Parnell finished fifth and was the only driver to score championship points in one of the V16s. The battle for victory was now well and truly joined between Alfa Romeo and Ferrari. Gonzalez broke Fangio's run of pole positions hustling his big Ferrari round in 1m 43.4s while Juan Manuel was second quickest one second slower than his fellow-countryman. Next up were Farina and Ascari putting two Ferraris and two Alfas on the front row. Behind them came Villoresi, Sanesi and Bonetto replacing Fagioli in the fourth Alfetta. Bonetto led first time round from Gonzalez, Farina, Ascari and Fangio but the burly Argentinean soon elbowed his way into the lead. Fangio quickly disposed of his rivals and went heel-for-leather after his fellow countryman. The battle for victory resolved itself into a spat between the two Argentineans and Farina who beat the old lap record. Juan Manuel went in front on lap 10 and stayed there until lap 39 when Gonzalez muscled past. The 159 then came in to refuel and with three-quarters of the race gone the Ferrari had a 1m 30s lead over the Alfa Romeo. Froilan then came in for a quick splash and dash which took twenty-three seconds and drove on to the chequered flag with over fifty seconds in hand over Fangio despite a desperate effort by the latter to catch him. Farina had dropped out when his car caught fire. On the

rostrum Juan Manuel, sporting as always, warmly congratulated Gonzalez. It was Ferrari's first victory in the F1 World Championship and Alfa Romeo's first significant defeat since the introduction of the F1 Grand Prix regulations in 1947. Thirteen years later Enzo Ferrari wrote in his memoirs a phrase that he knew would be repeated over and over again, "that day it was as if I had killed my mother!"

This kind of reflection was far from Fangio's mind; his sole aim was to harvest points knowing that from now on he was going to have his work cut out. After Silverstone he led the championship with 21 points followed by Farina with 15, Villoresi 12, Gonzalez 11 and Ascari 9. On the Nürburgring on 29th July the Ferraris in the hands of Ascari and Gonzalez set the two quickest times from Fangio's Alfa, on the Argentinean's first time out on the circuit, and

• **43**_14th July 1951: Ferrari scored their first F1 World Championship victory in the British Grand Prix on the Silverstone circuit. Gonzalez in his 375 is about to pass Fangio's 159 Alfa Romeo and head on to victory.

Farina. Juan Manuel went into an immediate lead but was soon passed by Ascari and when the latter refuelled Gonzalez took over first place. Alfa's challenge faded after Farina and Bonetto both retired, gearbox for the former and supercharger for the latter. The Milan factory had entrusted a fourth Alfetta to veteran Paul Pietsch who knew the circuit well but the German departed the race in a spectacular accident leaving Fangio alone to do battle with four Ferraris, as Villoresi and Taruffi were not far behind him. Victory went to the Scuderia but fortunately for the Argentinean the winner was Ascari, who fought hard for his well-deserved success finishing thirty seconds in front of the Alfa. Fangio added another seven points to his tally as he set fastest lap. He still led the championship with 28 points from Ascari now in second place with 17. Then came Farina with 15 after his pointless race in Germany tying with Gonzalez for third. Mathematically one of these three drivers could beat Fangio (and Ferrari Alfa Romeo) as there were still two rounds to go, the Italian and Spanish Grands Prix and because of the rules he had to drop his worst three results.

In the Bari Grand Prix on 2nd September Fangio beat Gonzalez and Taruffi in their Ferraris. The race did not count for the championship but it whipped up a storm of interest among journalists and spectators for the forthcoming Italian Grand Prix. On 16th September on the Monza circuit the stands were packed and tension was at its height. During testing Sanesi crashed and was burnt so De Graffenried was called in as a last minute replacement in the fourth Alfa. The four 375s were in the hands of the usual drivers and there were two other Ferraris entered, Peter Whitehead in his old 125 and Brazilian Chico Landi in a 2.6 litre model. Also making its debut was the 4.5 litre Osca in the hands of Franco Rol. The fast Monza circuit suited the Alfettas down to the ground and Fangio set pole in 1m 53.2s ahead of Farina 1m 53.9s, Ascari 1m 55.1s and Gonzalez 1m 55.9s. They were on the front row and on row 2 were Villoresi, Taruffi and Bonetto. The opening laps of the race were mind-boggling as the cars blasted their way round the circuit with Fangio going straight into the lead followed by Farina. Ascari fluffed his getaway but after only three laps he caught and passed the two

● **44**_In this photo taken at Monza before the Italian Grand Prix can be seen the Alfa Romeo team drivers, from left to right: Fangio, Farina, Bonetto and De Graffenried. Note the different footwear!

65

• **46**_A few laps later Fangio was to retire like Farina above. The smoke pouring from the bonnet indicates an oil leak. The Argentinean's retirement compromised his chances in the championship. But not fatally.

• **45**_Fangio flat-out in his Alfa Romeo is about to be caught by Ascari in the big Ferrari while a lumbering Lago Talbot keeps well out of the Italian's way.
(Centro di Doucumentazione Storice Alfa Romeo - William Huon archives)

Alfettas. This was not to be the Milan firm's day and on lap 7 came the first hint of trouble when Farina stopped with ignition problems. He restarted in Bonetto's car, which was in fifth place. Fangio had a rear tyre blow and stopped at his pit for a wheel change going back out in fifth. He really had to put the hammer down and doing something that was very rare for him over revved his engine, which gave up the ghost on lap 40 out of the 80 scheduled for the race. Gonzalez had got past Farina so the Ferraris were now running one-two with Ascari over two minutes ahead of his team-mate. The strain was also telling on the Ferrari engines and Ascari was forced to back off a little. Gonzalez came in for a quick stop allowing Farina up into second position but the latter was victim of the 159's excessive thirst and had to refuel ten laps before the end. Ascari took his second consecutive victory followed by Gonzalez making it a Ferrari double. In the championship Ascari now had

25 points with Gonzalez on 21. Fangio was still in the lead with 28 but under serious pressure from the Scuderia drivers.

Extreme tension reigned in the Ferrari and Alfa Romeo camps with one round left to go, exacerbated by the fact that the Spanish Grand Prix was on 28th October six weeks after Monza. This gave the engineers and drivers plenty of time to prepare the cars and settings and the journalists to work the Tifosi up into a frenzy. In Barcelona it was very hot on the day of the race. Pedralbes was partly a city circuit with the start and finish line on a very wide downward sloping avenue and overall spectator protection was non-existent. A touch of modernism was the fact that the cars were timed to within 100th of a second. The twenty starters were lined up in 4-3-4 formation with two cars on the last row. On pole was Ascari in 2m 10.59s followed by Fangio 2m 12.27s, Gonzalez 2m 14.61s, Farina 2m 15.67s and Villoresi 2m 16.38s. Ascari went into the lead

• **49**_On his return to Buenos Aires he was greeted by a frenzied crowd who had come to celebrate their F1 World Champion. It would not be the last time.
(Christian Moity - DR archives)

• **47 and 48**_Barcelona, Pedralbes on 28th October 1951. Fangio acknowledges the chequered flag as he scores a convincing victory in the Spanish Grand Prix, helped by Ferrari's monumental error. It was the first of the great Argentinean's legendary five F1 World Championship titles.

from Farina but by lap 4 Fangio had got past both of them. Thanks to its lower fuel consumption Ferrari had every chance of winning this race - and why not the championship - but a stupid mistake was to scupper its chances. At Spa the Alfa team had fitted bigger wheels on its cars at the last minute. This time it was the Scuderia which improvised by fitting its four cars with smaller diameter wheels to improve acceleration and better in-gear response. Also rumour had it that Alfa Romeo had fitted even larger fuel tanks on the Alfettas. In the race the Ferraris threw tyre treads with reckless abandon! Taruffi was the first to stop on lap 6 followed by Villoresi and Ascari on lap 8 and Gonzalez on lap 14. In the meantime the Alfettas of Fangio, Farina and

Bonetto were solidly installed in the first three places. Taruffi crashed after another tread flew off damaging the rim and Villoresi went out with deficient ignition. In their cars fitted with fresh rubber Ascari and Gonzalez did their best to catch the Alfas. They got past Bonetto and Froilan even managed to overtake Farina when the latter refuelled for the second time. Fangio had refuelled just before his team-mate and upped the pace in the closing laps to put himself out of reach of Gonzalez. Farina did the same and managed to save his third spot fending off Ascari who finished fourth. The Ferrari drivers were unable to follow the Alfas' rhythm, as they feared another blow out. And so Fangio crossed the finishing line to rapturous cheers to win the first of his five world championship titles. ■

Chapter 9
1952-1953
To hell and back

● **50**_Monza 13th September
1953: Fangio scored his only
Grand Prix victory of the 1953
season by winning the Italian
round of the world
championship in his Maserati
A6/SSG ending two years'
domination by the F2
Ferrari 500s.

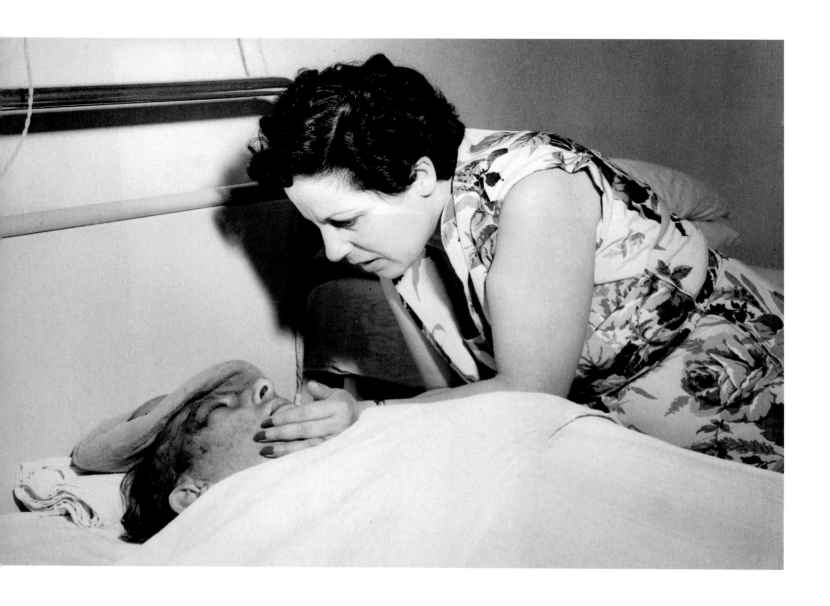

By winning the World Championship for Drivers Fangio immediately became a part of Argentinean legend like Jorge Luis Borges, the writer, and Carlos Gardel, father of the tango. His compatriots adored him and his business interests were flourishing in Buenos Aires and Balcarce thanks to the hard work of his brothers and associates. In the main his rivals on the track respected his talent and fair play even if some like Gonzalez (from 1951) were jealous of his success but he had no real enemies. He took advantage of the grants provided by the Peron government but avoided having his name associated with any form of political propaganda. Fangio's love life remains an enigma. He never married, had no children but had a constant companion, Dona Andreina Espinosa known as "Beba." In the European press they were presented as husband and wife but in Argentina it was a well-known fact that she was married to somebody else. Fangio certainly attracted the opposite sex and had liaisons with other women, the best-known being with a young

Belgian lady in 1951, who was a very talented rally driver. On the whole, though, he was basically a discrete person with little taste for luxury and above all very attached to his family and faithful to his friends. For example: he brought his father a present, chosen by the latter, a magnificent bike made by Bianchi in Italy. In 1951, Juan Manuel was forty years old and the best F1 racing driver in the world in an incredibly dangerous sport. He could easily have retired especially as Alfa Romeo had decided to stop Grand Prix racing. This decision was to have direct consequences on the future of the world championship. Talbot and Maserati had financial problems and Osca and BRM were still not ready so the CSI was not very happy about the possibility of a Ferrari walkover in Formula 1. BRM's decision to withdraw from the Turin Grand Prix was the final nail in the coffin. It was decided that the World Championship for Drivers would be run for Formula 2 cars as an interim measure in 1952-53. This would give the constructors time to prepare for the new F1 regulations that were due

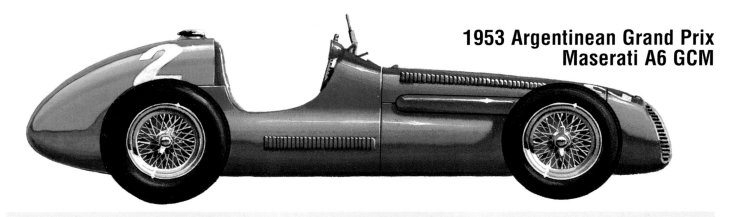

Designers: Vittorio Bellantani and Alberto Massimino

Engine
Make-Type: Maserati A6G
Number of cylinders/layout: Straight six (front)
Cubic capacity: 1959,5 ccs
Bore/stroke: 75 x 75 mm
Compression ratio: 12:1
Max. Power: 180 bhp
Max. Revs: 7500 rpm
Block: cast iron
Carburettors: 3 double barrel Webers
Distribution: D.O.H.C
Number of valves per cylinder: 2
Ignition: magneto (Marelli)

Transmission
Gearbox/speeds: Maserati longitudinal (5)
Clutch: Maserati

Chassis
Type: Twin tube ladder frame
Suspension: Independent with unequal length wishbones (front).
Live axle with tubular radius rods (rear)
Dampers: Helicoidal springs (front)
Transversal leaf springs (rear)
Wheels: Borani 6.00 x 15
Tyres: Pirelli
Brakes: Drums mounted in the wheels

Dimensions
Wheelbase: 2300 mm
Tracks: 1300 mm (front), 1240 mm (rear)
Weight: 580 kgs
Fuel tanks' capacity: 150 litres

Raced in Argentina.

to come into effect in 1954. The current crop of F1 cars had the right to race in non-championship Grands Prix and F. Libre events.

F2 was the training ground for future F1 drivers. It was a monoposto formula but unlike the modern single make F3000 each car had its own identity (engine, chassis, gearbox etc) and the current F1 stars did not hesitate to come and do battle with the newcomers in Grands Prix that were awarded international status. There were those who feared bargain basement races with less powerful cars (cubic capacity limited to 2 litres unsupercharged) but overall the Grands Prix were of a high level although Ferrari dominated until Maserati got its act together. The Cooper-Bristols also posed the occasional threat to the red cars while HWM and Gordini sometimes finished in the top six. Driverwise Mike Hawthorn was the quickest of the new generation beating Fangio in the memorable 1953 French Grand Prix on the Reims circuit.

For the 1952 season Juan Manuel had a full schedule which began with Formula Libre races in Brazil, Uruguay and Argentina in the ACA's supercharged Ferrari 166 after which he was supposed to begin his defence of his F1 crown in the new 6-cylinder works Maserati. He was down to drive for Alfa Romeo in endurance and in Formula 1 he contracted to BRM (British Racing Motors) based in Bourne. It was probably this overcharged schedule that caused the most serious accident of his career.

The 1952 season got off to a flying start for the new world champion. Between 13th January and 30th March he competed in seven races in a Ferrari: in Sao Paulo, Rio de Janeiro, Buenos Aires and Piriapolis. Then he returned to Europe stopping in England first of all where he tested the V16 BRM, which was originally financed by public subscription. It was very powerful "but a real challenge to drive", as Fangio said. Power only came in around 7000 rpm, which required footwork on the clutch that would have done credit to a ballet dancer just to get the thing going! There was an enormous surge up to 11 000 rpm with the engine note rising to a banshee-like shriek which would stick in the memory of other drivers such as Moss, Wharton, Gonzalez etc. The other problem was that the ill-designed chassis lacked rigidity so that even on the straight it was difficult to keep the car on the track! In these conditions Fangio amazed the BRM engineers and mechanics present at the test on the Silverstone circuit. His calm, precise approach meant that he was one of the few who dared exploit the full potential of this diabolical machine. He was supposed to drive it at Goodwood on 14th April but it was not ready (!). Fangio had no seat and John Cooper had a Cooper-Bristol available for the Chichester Cup. The Argentinean accepted the drive - without payment - something that Cooper talked about till the end of his days, but the car was not properly set up and Fangio could do no better than sixth.

He then went back to his Milan base and rejoined his friends. Alfa Romeo gave him a 1900 saloon for the Mille Miglia on 4th May. Helped by Sala he came home 22nd overall out of over 500 starters. While awaiting the opening round of the world championship put back because of cancellations, he went to the Planques circuit in Albi to drive a BRM in a Formula Libre Grand Prix backed up by Ken Wharton. Both cars retired with

mechanical problems. On Saturday 7th June the Ulster Trophy was held on the Dundrod circuit in Northern Ireland. Again BRM entered two cars for Fangio and Stirling Moss but both dark green cars retired due to overheating (Moss) and fuel starvation (Fangio).

The next day (Sunday 8th June) the Monza circuit was the theatre of the Grand Prix de l'Autodromo and also the debut of the new Maserati A6GCM powered by a 2-litre 6-cylinder D.O.H.C engine designed by Colombo who had joined the Bologna firm after leaving Alfa Romeo. Fangio could not miss this event, as it would be his first drive in the car with which he was to defend his title. In addition, he had given his word to the Orsi brothers.

Prince Bira had a private plane and he had promised Fangio to take him from Belfast to Milan after the race. Bira crashed out on the first lap and forgetting his promise took off for Italy without waiting for the Argentinean. Fangio found a flight to London for himself and Louis Rosier and then another to Paris. There were no planes from Orly to Milan because of fog so Rosier then offered to drive Fangio to Lyon in his Renault Fregate and when they arrived there he lent him his car to continue on to Monza. It was a generous gesture on the part of the Frenchman who lived in Clermont-Ferrand, as he was not driving in Italy. The Argentinean set off alone on the "route du

• **52**_18th January 1953: The start of the Argentinean Grand Prix on the new 17th October circuit. Ascari's Ferrari and the Maseratis of Fangio and Gonzalez were destined to retire.

• **53**_25th April 1953: Fangio partnered by Sala gave the Italian public something to cheer about in the Mille Miglia. He finished second overall in his Alfa Romeo Disco Volante coupe despite skewed steering, which probably cost him victory.
(Centro Di Documentazione Storice Alfa Romeo – Christian Moity Archives)

• **54**_31st May 1953: The BRM team's V16s before the start of the Albi Grand Prix. Fangio and Gonzalez were part of the driver line-up with Juan Manuel winning the first heat.
(Auto-Passion archives – DR)

Mont Cenis"- there was no Mont Blanc tunnel at the time - and here he takes up the story. "I couldn't take part in practice but the organisers, with the agreement of the other drivers, allowed me to start on the back row. I arrived at Monza at 14h00 totally exhausted. At 14h30 I was on the grid and on lap 1 I passed several cars. By 15h00 I was in the hospital!"

Fangio remembered his accident. On lap 2 on the exit from Lesmo he went off-line onto the side of the track and being too tired he did not correct the slide quickly enough. The Maserati hit a straw bale, reared up into the air throwing out its driver. He saw the tops of the trees, smelt the fresh grass on which he landed and then lost consciousness.

Later he found a gash in his helmet showing that this piece of equipment, which had become obligatory since the start of the 1952 season, had saved his life. In the hospital lesions to his vertebrae were diagnosed: he was put in traction for six days and then encased in plaster. Farina and Frenchman André Simon, first and second in the race driving Ferraris, sneaked in to see him in the hospital and gave him their laurels. Although only half-conscious he recognised them and both drivers were really taken aback! Juan Manuel remained corseted up to his neck for three months and had many visitors. Among his racing driver friends Felice Bonetto was the one who came to see him the most and this led to a deep friendship

• **55**_A smiling quartet just
before the Dutch Grand Prix at
Zandvoort; left to right: Ascari,
Fangio, Farina and Villoresi.

developing between the two men. Another visitor
was Giuseppe Busso, the Alfa Romeo engineer,
who showed him plans of the Tipo 160, a single-
seater that he was planning for the forthcoming
2.5 litre formula. It was technically a daring design
including a flat 12 engine with an integrated
gearbox and a driving position very far to the rear.
Fangio was very interested but unfortunately the
Tipo 160 never got beyond the drawing board.

He left hospital in September and could
move around provided he took care. He was able
to turn the upper part of his body but not his
head and in this condition gave the start of the
Italian Grand Prix won by Alberto Ascari who was
crowned 1952 World Champion. Gonzalez in a
Maserati finished second in the race. Obviously the
season was a disaster for Fangio but at the end of
the year after a month's rest in Argentina where
the country was mourning the death of Eva Peron,
he got ready to start racing again. In Buenos Aires
he asked Juan Galvez to lend him the Alfa

Romeo 308 belonging to his brother, Oscar, in
which the former now raced. Although the test
was short it was enough to convince him that he
had recovered his automatic reflexes and physical
faculties.

The 1953 season was one of Fangio's busiest
if not the most successful. It proved to him and to
others that he was still as quick as ever and he
soon found himself back on the topmost step of
the rostrum. It was the best possible preparation
for what was to be the most glorious part of his
brilliant career. He raced in the world
championship (still run to F2 rules) in a Maserati.
Alongside him in the Trident team were fellow-
countrymen Froilan Gonzalez (released by Ferrari)
and the young and very promising Onofre
Marimon. Fangio sponsored his European debut, as
he was Domingo Marimon'son, Fangio's old rival in
the "Turismo de Carreteras" events. Juan Manuel
also drove for BRM and in sports cars he raced for
Alfa Romeo then Lancia.

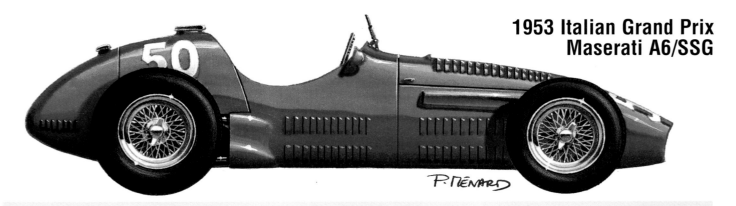

Designer: Gioacchino Colombo

Engine

Make/type: Maserati
Number of cylinders/layout: straight 6 (front)
Cubic capacity: 1997 ccs
Bore/stroke: 76.2 x 72 mm
Compression ratio: 13.7 to 1
Max. power: 190 bhp
Max. Revs: 7500 rpm
Block: cast iron
Carburettors: 3 double barrel Webers
Distribution: D.O.H.C
Number of valves per cylinder: 2
Ignition: magneto (Marelli)

Transmission

Gearbox/no. of ratios: Maserati longitudinal (5)
Clutch: Maserati

Chassis

Type: Twin tube ladder frame
Suspension: Independent (front) live axle (rear)
Dampers: Telescopic – transversal leaf spring (rear)
Wheels: Borani 6.00 x 15
Tyres: Pirelli
Brakes: drums mounted in the wheels

Dimensions

Wheelbase: 2300 mm
Tracks: 1300 mm (front) 1240 mm (rear)
Dry weight: 580 kgs
Fuel tank capacity: 150 litres

Used in Holland and Italy.

The season began with the Argentinean Grand Prix on the new 17th October track, an ultra-modern complex some forty kilometres from Buenos Aires, inaugurated with great pomp and ceremony by the Peron regime on 18th January 1953. It was the first time that Argentina was included in the world champion and in addition, the country was hosting the opening round. Alas, the race was to end in tragedy. There was a huge crowd (the figure of 400 0000 was quoted) massed around the track in a state of extreme excitement at the prospect of seeing their heroes, Fangio above all, but also Gonzalez and Marimon, doing battle with the best drivers in the world especially those in the Ferraris. In one of those theatrical gestures that would not have been out of place in the "panem et circenses" of ancient Rome, Peron allowed the organisers to lower the barriers around the track. The spectators, who were still as rash as in 1949 when Wimille had been killed, crowded around the edge of the circuit and sat on the verges. Regardless of the danger the cars were unleashed. Fangio was at the wheel of the latest Maserati A6 GCM which was said to put out 180 bhp for a weight of 580 kgs as opposed to the Ferrari's 600 kgs but the latter's fuel consumption was better. He set pole and during the opening laps was hot on the wheels of Ascari and Farina in their Ferraris. Tragedy struck on lap 32 when Farina swerved to avoid a child crossing the track and his car scythed down several spectators. In the ensuing panic an ambulance also went into the crowd. Nine people died but the race was not stopped! Fangio retired a few laps later with broken transmission and victory went to Ascari.

After the non-championship Buenos Aires Grand Prix on 1st February in which Fangio was again let down by his car, he flew to Europe. He drove in the Mille Miglia on 26th April with Giulio Sala in the new 3.6 litre Alfa Romeo Disco Volante three of which with coupe bodywork were entered by the Milan company. Fangio was to show other

● **56**_Reims 5th July 1953.
The start of one of the most
thrilling Grands Prix in F1
history. Into the lead goes
Gonzalez in his Maserati
(no.20) ahead of Fangio's sister
car (no.18). Mike Hawthorn, the
winner, is back in 7th place.

facets of his talent in this very demanding race, his
ability to combine caution, cunning and calculated
risk. During the race he discovered by accident that
the chassis had broken at the front in the place
where the steering box was mounted. The result
was that it worked when he turned left but when
he turned right the car went straight on. Fangio
and his co-driver were determined to carry on and
asked the Alfa Romeo service crew at the stop in
Bologna if they had an arc-welding machine. No
was the answer and making sure that the
mechanics did not look under the bonnet, as they
were afraid they would be told to stop, they
continued. Fangio drove by cutting the right-hand
corners as the cambered verge kept the damaged
wheel pointing in the right direction. They were in
the lead after Florence but in the final stage, which
they covered at over 160 km/h, Giannino Marzotto
passed them in his big 4.1 litre Ferrari. It was an

amazing feat and dissipated whatever doubts
Fangio might have had about his skills. He drove
the Disco Volantes again on several occasions but
without much success. In the Le Mans 24 Hours he
retired in the car shared with Marimon and it was
the same story in the Spa 24 Hours this time with
Sanesi as co-driver. He scored one victory in the
open version in the Supercortemaggiore in
September.

After the Mille Miglia Fangio went to
Bordeaux to drive a new 2-litre Gordini for his
friend Amédée who had just been dropped by
Simca. The 'wizard' wanted to go it alone with new
6 and 8 cylinder models and he needed some
publicity. Juan Manuel finished third in this non-
championship Grand Prix and then he travelled to
Naples to rejoin the Maserati team. He came
second on the Posillipo circuit and third in the
Targa Florio after taking over Sergio Mantovani's

car (the latter was tenth at the time). It was the end of action-packed May. On 1st June he was in Albi with the BRM team to compete in a Formula Libre race and battling with Ascari's Ferrari he gave the English team one of its best results. He finished first in his heat beating an exhausted Ascari but in the second his car began to throw tyre treads forcing him to retire.

The next round of the world championship was the Dutch Grand Prix on the Zandvoort circuit on 7th June. Fangio managed to split the Ferraris of Ascari and Farina but again he was let down by the Maserati's transmission.

After the Le Mans 24 Hours he found himself back at Spa for the Belgian Grand Prix on 21st June. To say he was thirsting for revenge would be an understatement! He set a brilliant pole position in 4m 30s beating Ascari and Gonzalez (4m 32s) and this time Ascari's Ferrari found itself the meat in a Maserati sandwich. The Italian was obliged to call on all his skills because it was evident that the rivalry between the two Argentineans had weakened their friendship and each one was now out for himself. Gonzalez was no longer in Fangio's shadow and had proved that he was as quick as his fellow-countryman. The early laps saw a bitter

• **57**_Hawthorn and Fangio side by side at over 250 km/h on the straight going down to Thillois during their epic struggle. Mike is laughing behind his visor as the Argentinean gives him a quick glance. Afterwards the Englishman said he could read the Maserati's rev counter!

• **58**_The mind-boggling finish of the French Grand Prix. Hawthorn leans forward urging his Prancing Horse on just beating the Maserati by one of the tiniest margins ever in the history of F1 after a battle lasting some two-and-a-half hours.

• **59**_15th July 1953. A beautiful shot of Fangio in the V16 BRM on the Silverstone circuit where he came second in the Formula Libre race run before the British Grand Prix. It was a very difficult car to drive due to poor road holding and a very narrow rev band. The sound of its engine is one of the most beautiful in the history of racing but "it was a real challenge to drive" in the words of Fangio, one of the few drivers who tamed its awesome power.

• **60**_The tubby Gonzalez squeezes into his Maserati during practice for the British Grand Prix. Just behind and to his right Fangio in suit and tie watches the mechanics as they change the plugs on his A6/SSG.

struggle between the two drivers which turned to Froilan's advantage as he led the race until lap 10 when he was 16 seconds in front of Juan Manuel, himself 39 ahead of Ascari who had left the other Ferraris far behind. It couldn't last and the high-speed battle soon took its toll. Just after beating the lap record Gonzalez's accelerator broke on lap 11 and two laps later Fangio's engine blew. Ascari found himself in the lead from Hawthorn, Farina and Villoresi all Ferrari-mounted. There was still a long way to go as the Grand Prix's distance was 508 km. Marimon passed Villoresi's Ferrari and Belgian Johnny Claes was called in to hand over to Fangio. The latter rejoined and passed

De Graffenried and Trintignant to take fifth place on lap 25. By now Farina had retired and Hawthorn was in trouble. Juan Manuel saw a rostrum finish looming and maybe even a win even though Ascari was firmly installed in the lead. He launched an attack on Villoresi for second place but on the last lap he pushed too hard in the Stavelot corner which was taken at around 180 km/h. He spun, hit one side of the track and then the other and was slightly injured in the accident. If anything, this incident strengthened his resolve even more.

Two weeks later drivers and cars arrived at the Reims circuit for the French Grand Prix. The famous track in the champagne region had been modified and lengthened and now measured just over 8,3 km. It no longer went through the Gueux village and followed a series of sweeping curves to the Muizon hairpin. Then came a long straight going up towards the old Garenne corner and from there the cars raced downwards to Thillois. Thanks to this layout slipstreaming was to play a very important role in the Grand Prix. It also made for a very exciting event with frequent changes among the leading group, increased the average speed and gave the cars a terrible hammering under the burning sun.

The 1953 French Grand Prix will remain engraved in the memories of all those fortunate enough to see it as one of the greatest races ever. Osca's comeback and the presence of the usual English teams like Cooper-Bristol, Connaught and HWM plus Behra in his Gordini, who was hoping to repeat his previous year's win on the same circuit, were of little interest to the huge crowd massed around the circuit come to see another round in the battle between Ferrari and Maserati. They were not to be disappointed.

A festive ambience reigned as Toto Roche unleashed the twenty-five cars and Gonzalez shot through from the second row, which he shared with Fangio, to take the lead. The burly Argentinean soon opened up a gap over his pursuers as at Spa. Behind came a gaggle of roaring, snarling racing cars driven by Hawthorn, Ascari, Villoresi, Farina, Bonetto, a newcomer to the Maserati team, and Fangio engaged in a wheel-to-wheel battle. Juan Manuel then got into his stride and picked off the Ferraris one by one setting a

• 63 to 67_Monza
13th September 1953: The Italian Grand Prix was almost more thrilling than the Reims event two months previously. These five photos bear eloquent witness to the intensity of the battle between the Ferrari and Maserati drivers: Farina in no.6, Ascari in no.4, Fangio in no.50 and Marimon in no.54. Finally, victory went to Fangio. In this era the photographers really were in the thick of the action!

new lap record as he blasted past Farina. Gonzalez in the meantime had stopped to refuel, and by half-distance Fangio was in the lead with Mike Hawthorn glued to his tail. Their battle was to last thirty-two laps with them swapping places several times per lap as they pulled away from their rivals. Hawthorn said afterwards that they were so close flat out side by side on the run down to Thillois that on several occasions they glanced at each other and he could read the Maserati's rev counter! In the final lap on the exit from Thillois Mike had his car in first gear and gave it full throttle while Fangio's was in second and a bit slower of the mark. As they roared down to the start/finish line the Argentinean was clawing back those few centimetres that separated him from the Ferrari

but Hawthorn held on to score his first win by a whisker in a thrilling Grand Prix becoming the first Englishman to triumph in an F1 world championship race.

After some rest and relaxation Juan Manuel scored an easy victory in a Swiss hill climb (Vue des Alpes) in his Maserati and then found himself back in the thick of Grand Prix racing. Fangio was far and away the quickest of the Maserati drivers, as proved again by his second places on the Silverstone and Nurburgring circuits, but he was unable to break the Ferrari stranglehold or threaten Ascari for the world championship even though the latter retired in Germany after setting the fastest lap as victory went to Farina. In Switzerland Ascari won again while Fangio took over Bonetto's car and came in fourth.

On 30ᵗʰ August there was a 1000 km endurance event on the Nürburgring counting for the newly-created Sports Car World Championship. After Alfa Romeo's withdrawal Fangio shared one of the three works D 24 Lancias with Bonetto but retired with a broken fuel pump.

Then came the Italian Grand Prix, the final round of the world championship. Although Ascari had the title in his pocket (his second) and Gonzalez was missing after an accident in Portugal - he did not race in the last three Grands Prix of the season - Maserati and Ferrari were each desperate to triumph in front of their home crowd. Fangio was determined to win and to break his run of bad luck at Monza since his historic victory there in 1949. Thirty cars started including six Ferraris, the four regulars plus Maglioli and Carini. In Gonzalez's absence Maserati entrusted its fourth car to Sergio Mantovani. Ascari again set pole from Fangio and Farina. Behind the three world champions Marimon, Hawthorn and Villoresi were on row 2. When the flag fell Ascari went into the lead followed by Farina and Marimon who managed to split the two Ferraris justifying the confidence placed in him by Maserati and Fangio. He drove a fantastic race until lap 46 when he had to stop with a damaged oil radiator losing two laps to the leading group, which he rejoined after his stop. The battle for victory now raged between the two Ferraris and Fangio's Maserati the cars

swapping positions several times each lap. Juan Manuel dropped back to give himself a breathing space, then set the fastest lap and caught the two Italians. The Maserati was quicker in a straight line but the Ferraris had better torque and acceleration out of the corners. As they roared into the Parabolica for the last time Ascari and Farina were side by side. Suddenly the world champion spun to avoid a backmarker. Farina went for the outside and Marimon hit Ascari. Fangio nipped through on the inside and took the chequered flag and second place in the title chase. It was Ferrari's first world championship defeat for two years. The following Sunday he won the Modena Grand Prix for Maserati. He then drove his last race for BRM, the Woodcote Trophy, in which he came second.

Just as Fangio was about to leave for Argentina he received an offer from Lancia through Felice Bonetto to drive one of the D 24 6 cylinder sports cars that the Turin Company had entered for the Carrera Panamerica in Mexico. He accepted straight away. After a few weeks' rest in Balcarce he joined the Lancia team in Tuxtla Gutierrez before the start. The race was run for the first time in 1950 and victory went to an Oldsmobile followed by two Cadillacs, specially tuned saloons that harked back to the "Carrateras" in which Fangio had cut his teeth. In 1951, victory went to Ferrari and in 1952 it was the turn of Mercedes-Benz with their new 300 SL. The race

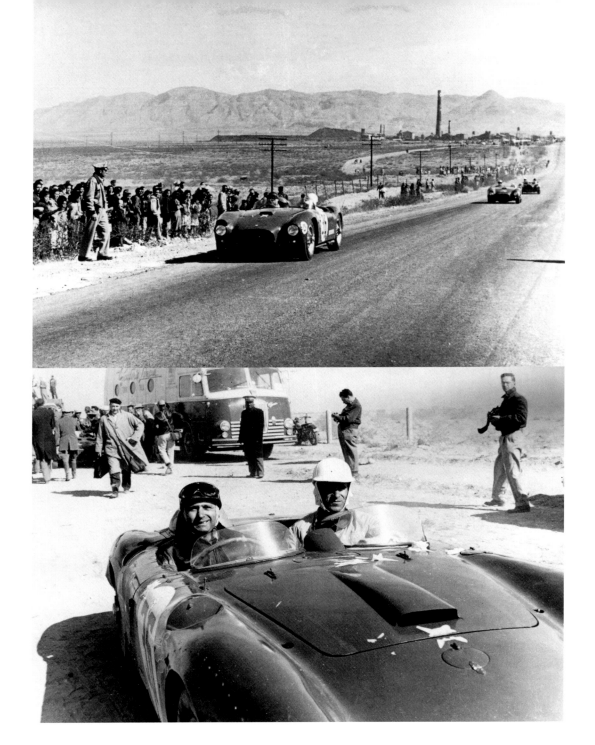

● **69 and 70_**
November 1953: Fangio at the
finish of the Carrera
Panamerica against the
backdrop of the splendid
Mexican countryside. He won
the race leading a Lancia triple
overshadowed by Felice
Bonetto's death.
(William Huon archives)

received enormous publicity in Mexico and the
USA combining as it did the conditions of the
Gran Premio road races of Latin America, the
drivers and cars of the Mille Miglia plus the locals
and a few North Americans. The event was all the
more important for the Europeans as it was part
of the Sports Car World Championship. The Lancia
armada consisted of five D 24 sports cars for
Fangio, Taruffi, Bonetto, Bracco and young
Eugenio Castellotti and also entered were Talbots,
Gordinis and Ferraris. The total distance of the
race was 3094 kms divided up into eight stages to
be covered between 19th and 23rd November. From
the start Fangio let his team-mates battle it out
among themselves while keeping ahead of the

Ferraris. Bonetto won the first stage and Taruffi
the next two and Maglioli the fourth all at
mind-blowing speed. It was in this stage that
tragedy struck the Lancia team as Bonetto, in hot
pursuit of Taruffi, was killed when he lost control
of his Lancia which went off and hit a post on the
entrance to the old Aztec town of Silea. A young
spectator told Fangio the news at the end of the
stage. Juan Manuel was very upset as he had lost
a dear friend. Gianni Lancia decided to continue
and at his request the Argentinean agreed to take
a mechanic on board. Bonetto's death cast a
shadow over Lancia's triple with overall victory
going to Fangio who had not won a single
stage! ∎

Chapter 10
1954
Return of the 3-pointed star

In the autumn of 1953 the world of motor racing was agog with the news of Mercedes-Benz's imminent return to racing. The German company had already tested the waters in 1952 with the 3 litre 6 cylinder 300 SLs that had won the Le Mans 24 Hours and the Carrera Panamericana, a grand touring version of which was about to go on sale. Mercedes-Benz's return

to Grand Prix racing, now run under the 2.5 litre formula, took shape in the spring of 1954. The men in the "Rennabteilung" the Daimler Benz competitions department directed by Fritz Nallinger backed up by the engineers Rudolf Uhlenhaut and Hans Scherenberg designed what at first sight appeared to be a very avant-garde racing car. It was powered by a straight 8 engine with desmodromic valve gear and direct fuel injection. The block and gearbox made ample use of magnesium and the car was enclosed in streamlined bodywork that hid the wheels, in-board drum brakes etc. Actually, a closer look revealed the fact that the solutions were not all that avant-gardist but rather the optimisation of tested formulas that, with the exception of fuel injection, would not be seen again in Formula 1. The latter came from technology used on the Messerschmitt fighters during World War II and replaced the traditional carburettors. Probably inspired by Mercedes-Benz its use became widespread from the 60s onwards. However, the domination that the German company was to exercise during the next two years in Grand Prix racing was down to its financial and technical resources, a very reliable racing car whether in F1 or sports car trim (the W 196 and the 3 litre 300 SLR) helped by the fact that its rivals were in disarray, plus a competitions department that was managed with exemplary rigour and professionalism. The German works team was placed under the iron rule of one Alfred Neubauer who, in the 30s, had held the same post when the Nazi government kept a close eye on motor racing as it was one of their propaganda vehicles. Like Enzo Ferrari whom he held in high esteem (and vice versa) Neubauer had been a racing driver in the 20s. He took up the job of team manager when he and his employers realised that his true talent lay in his capacity to lead and to get the very best out of both men and machines. His iron-fisted authority did not exclude a real affection for his drivers as well as his enormous capacity (almost as big as his stomach on which rested his collection of stopwatches) to enjoy the good things of life, especially on the evening of a victory. He was a very colourful character but a redoubtably efficient one. Another of the key men in the "Rennabteilung" was Rudolf Ulenhaut who had designed and developed the 1937 W 125 then the 1938-39 W 154s/W 163s. In addition, he was able to drive his cars as quickly and as well as the team regulars and knew the formidable Nürburgring - among other circuits - like the back of his hand. He was greatly respected by his drivers, as they knew they were speaking to an equal to whom lying about a car's behaviour was useless.

● **71**_4ᵗʰ July 1954: The Mercedes-Benz mechanics push a very concentrated Fangio in his W 196 streamliner to his place on the starting grid for the French Grand Prix.

Neubauer had had his eye on Fangio since 1951 when he had entrusted him with one of the 1939 W 163s for the Argentinean Temporada. They met up again at Monza in 1953 and negotiations had gone on until the start of 1954 with the help of Baron Von Korff, a German go-between in Buenos Aires. In February a draft contract had been handed to Fangio just before his departure for Sebring in Florida where he was down to drive a Lancia D24 in the 12 Hour race. Lancia, of course, was working on its own F1 project and Juan Manuel was a likely candidate for a seat so in Stuttgart negotiations were speeded up. Neubauer was not exactly sure how many W 196 single-seaters would be built but the one thing he wanted was to have the Argentinean as his number 1 driver so he convinced Nallinger to postpone the sports car programme - supposed to start with the Mille Miglia - until 1955. This ensured that he would be able to guarantee Fangio a car for the French

Grand Prix on the Reims circuit and the six remaining F1 World Championship Grands Prix. On 20th March the Argentinean duly signed his contract with the German company. It was a very good deal for him as in addition to a comfortable salary he had the right to 90% of both starting and prize money, and all his expenses (hotel, food, plane tickets for himself and his companion) were paid by Mercedes-Benz. He had a company car, a top of the range 300S saloon followed by a 300 SL. In exchange he undertook to drive exclusively for Mercedes-Benz and take part in numerous test sessions. Finally, he agreed to participate in various promotional activities such as meeting the press, dealers etc. In this way and even if the amount of money in question bears no resemblance to that floating around today the contracts between the German company and its drivers prefigured modern practice. Backing up Fangio, who had had a clause inserted in his contract stating that no other Argentinean driver

Despite Herrmann's retirement the Mercedes-Benz's demonstration left the pundits gob-smacked. First race, first victory plus a double. The mythic P3 Alfa Romeo had done the same in the early 30s. However, during the next race the British Grand Prix on the Silverstone circuit on 17ᵗʰ July, it all went wrong for the German team. Again Fangio was on pole followed by Gonzalez and Hawthorn in their Ferraris and Moss's Maserati 250F. These four shared the front row and behind them on the second were Salvadori's Maserati 250F, Kling's Mercedes-Benz and Behra's Gordini who had all set the same time. In the race itself the silver cars were handicapped by their weight, the inefficiency of their Continental tyres in relation to the Pirellis when it began to rain and the drivers inability to sight the corners properly due to the all-enveloping bodywork. Fangio in his pursuit of the leaders Gonzalez, Moss, Hawthorn and then

Marimon spent a lot of time playing skittles with the cans used to mark the circuit edges destroying his car's pristine appearance in the process. His gearbox also played up so fourth place was about as much as he could hope for. Kling finished seventh. Victory went to his burly compatriot, Gonzalez followed by Hawthorn giving Ferrari an unexpected double while the promising Marimon came home third after setting the fastest lap, a brief glimpse of an all-too-ephemeral talent.

Given the financial and technical means at their disposal Mercedes-Benz reacted quickly to the Silverstone debacle. As their home Grand Prix was the next round of the championship there was no question of risking defeat on the mythic Nürburgring. The team arrived at the circuit with a new, lighter (60 kgs) version of the W 196 with conventional bodywork for Fangio, Kling and Lang while Herrmann had to make do with a

● **82**_22nd August 1954: Swiss
Grand Prix. Here Fangio is
pursued by Gonzalez in his
Ferrari, which he drove into
second place 57 secs behind
the Mercedes-Benz.
*(Daimler-Benz – William Huon
archives)*

streamliner. Practice was overshadowed by Onofre
Marimon's fatal accident. 'Pinocchio' as he was
called lost control of his Maserati in the
Wehrseifen, overturned and was killed instantly.
Fangio and Gonzalez rushed to the scene of the
accident and fell into each other's arms in tears,
reconciled by their fellow-countryman's death.
Marimon adored the 'Ring and probably lost
control trying to put in a very quick lap. Maserati
withdrew its cars as a sign of respect and Fangio
wanted to stand down but the inflexible
Neubauer ordered him to race. Gonzalez started
but soon handed over to Hawthorn. Juan Manuel
was again on pole with Hawthorn and Moss
alongside him and the Argentinean dominated
the race winning from the Gonzalez/Hawthorn
Ferrari but there were few smiles on the rostrum.
Kling finished fourth and set fastest lap.

Three weeks later in the Swiss Grand Prix
(incidentally the last on home soil) the main
opposition to the German cars again came from
the pugnacious Gonzalez who split the Mercedes
of Fangio and Herrmann, the young German
finishing third. Next round was the Italian Grand
Prix on the very fast Monza circuit so Mercedes
entered the streamlined version of the W 196.
Even if Fangio finally won by a lap from
Hawthorn's Ferrari wrapping up his second world
championship title, it was not as easy a victory as
it looked. On the front row with him were Ascari,
still on loan to Ferrari from Lancia, and Stirling
Moss. Ascari was in front for part of the race but
the real hard luck story was Moss. The Englishman
passed Fangio and opened out a commanding
lead until his engine blew on lap 68. Fastest lap
went to Gonzalez who took over Maglioli's car.

The final round of the world championship was the Spanish Grand Prix in Barcelona on 24th October and the main talking point was the appearance of the Lancia D 50, two of which were entered for Ascari and Villoresi. Designed by the famous Vittorio Jano, father of the P2 and P3 Alfa Romeos they were squat, purposeful looking little cars with the 90° V8 engine acting as a structural chassis member which helped explain the low centre of gravity and the position of the drive shaft running alongside the driver. Their pannier tanks gave more consistent road holding as they emptied, and the reason why so much weight was concentrated within the wheelbase was because it was supposed to provide better road holding. Which it did but there were a few problems sorting the car out. All in all it was a beautiful looking little machine in which Acari set pole ahead of Fangio. He led during the opening laps indicating that Mercedes would not have it all its own way in 1955 (alas, it was not to be the case). Villoresi went out on lap 2 with brake failure and on lap 10 Ascari retired with a slipping clutch. Hawthorn scored his second Grand Prix victory from Luigi Musso's Maserati while Fangio could do no better than third after paper blocked his car's radiator causing his engine to overheat. ■

• **83**_An official team photo signed by the members before the 1954 Italian Grand Prix. From left to right: Herrmann Lang, Alfred Neubauer the team manager, Juan Manuel Fangio, Karl Kling and Hans Herrmann. *(Daimler-Benz Pfeil – Christian Moity archives)*

Chapter 11
1955
A black year
Third title

Stirling Moss:
"Nobody knew his limits"

Stirling Moss is particularly well placed to assess Fangio, as he was his rival for several years and his team-mate at Mercedes-Benz in 1955. During a long interview in his home for the magazine Fanauto in 1986, he said the following:

"From him I learned self-control and when following him I had complete trust. We were called 'The Train' especially when we were in our two Mercedes and I was only a metre behind. I observed his line and from it I tried to judge my own. Fangio's greatness resided in the fact that he went only as quickly as necessary, but nobody knew his limit. I especially remember a Monaco practice session: Fangio had set a time and immediately afterwards I went much quicker. He went out again and beat my time. I think it must have happened about fifteen times like this and each time he just knocked that fraction off. He also combined precision, endurance and speed."

● **92**_Fangio and Moss play follow-my-leader on the exit from the Portier corner. A Mercedes double looked assured until!

● **93**_5th June 1955: A beautiful view of the magnificent Spa-Francorchamps circuit during the Belgian Grand Prix. In the background can be seen the Raidillon and Eau Rouge while Fangio rounds the La Source hairpin in his W 196.
(Photo Daimler-Benz – William Huon archives)

● **94**_Fangio flat out up the Raidillon. His driving that day left many observers open-mouthed with admiration including Paul Frère who finished 4th.

Paul Frère:
"His class as a driver plus the car"

In the 1955 Belgian Grand Prix I drove a Ferrari Squalo. I remember the briefing on Sunday morning with Ugolini and all the drivers. I was always stuck by Fangio's calm. He said little but when he did it was worth listening to. I didn't see much of him in the race as he disappeared off into the distance with Moss on his tail. There are those who say that Fangio often had easy victories because he had the best car. I find it normal that the best driver of an era has the best car. I would say that the W 196 Mercedes - a car that I tested later - was the best F1 in 1954 and 55 but you had to get used to it. It was more powerful than the others but heavier. Why Fangio was so successful in Grand Prix was more because of his skills as a driver than the car. It was a combination of the two. The comparison with Moss in 1955 is not really valid as they never had to push their cars to the limit."

and was killed. His death left a huge hole in the world of motor racing as he was much liked and respected by everybody. Unfortunately, there was still worse to come.

Fangio then won the Eifel race in a 300 SLR and on 5th June at Spa the two W 196s scored another double in the Belgian Grand Prix from Farina and Paul Frère's Super Squalo Ferraris. Their only real threat came from Castellotti's Lancia as he managed to persuade Gianni Lancia to enter at least one car for Spa as a kind of homage to his mentor, Ascari, notwithstanding the company's dire financial situation. He put the D 50 on pole and led for a few laps before the crown wheel broke. Thus Fangio cruised on to an easy victory setting fastest lap.

Rarely has the Le Mans 24 Hour race had such an exceptional entry list as that for the 1955 event. Jaguar and Aston Martin were there to defend British Racing Green against the red Ferraris and Maseratis and above all the silver Mercedes-Benz, the hot favourites after their win in the Mille Miglia. In practice the 300 SLRs tested their new pop up air brake which helped slow the cars more quickly in high speed braking zones. The factory entered three cars for Fangio-Moss, Kling-Simon and Levegh-Fitch. American John Fitch had had a lot of experience in big sports cars like the Cunningham while Pierre Levegh was an endurance regular who had come within a hair's breadth of winning the 1952 24 Hours in his Talbot. He led until the

• **95**_11th June 1955: Kling (no.21) and Fangio (no.19) in their 300 SLRs in the 24 Hour race just before tragedy intervened. They are followed by Trintignant's Ferrari (no.5) who took up the chase when Castellotti's car fell back after mixing it with Hawthorn's Jaguar and the Mercedes for the lead.

twenty-third hour and greatly impressed Neubauer. The German team manager probably received some discrete pressure from the French Mercedes-Benz importer to include him in the team.

The first two hours of the race run in sunny weather in front of a huge crowd saw a no-holds-barred battle between Castellotti's 4.4 litre Ferrari, Hawthorn's D-Type Jaguar and Fangio's Mercedes-Benz. The Italian then lost ground and the Englishman and the Argentinean went at it hammer and tongs as if they were in a Formula 1 Grand Prix. Around 18h20 tragedy struck. Hawthorn suddenly realised he did not have enough fuel for an extra lap (13,492 km) braked hard and pulled over into the pit lane (at that

time there was no separation between it and the track) to stop and refuel. Englishman Lance Macklin seeing the Jaguar cutting in in front of him slammed on the brakes and swerved left. This happened in front of the main grandstands where the track was narrow and bordered by fences. Travelling at over 250 km/h Levegh's Mercedes burst on the scene. The Frenchman was unable to avoid the Austin-Healey and took off over the back of the English car. His 300 SLR landed on the bank and exploded and its engine cut a swathe through the crowd killing over eighty people and injured around two hundred. The Clerk of the Course, the very experienced Charles Faroux, kept his head and decided not to stop the race. It was not done out of cynicism but rather to guarantee

1955 Belgian Grand Prix
Mercedes-Benz W 196

P. MÉNARD

Designer: Rudolf Uhlenhaut

Engine
Make/type Mercedes-Benz
Number of cylinders: straight 8 (front)
Cubic capacity: 2496 ccs
Bore/stroke: 76 x 68.8 mm
Compression ratio: 12.5: 1
Max. power: 290 bhp
Max. Revs: 8500 rpm
Block: steel
Injection; direct (Bosch)
Distribution: D.O.H.C.
Number of valves per cylinder: 2 (Desmodromic command)
Ignition: magneto (Bosch)
Number of plugs per cylinder: 2
Weight: 204 kgs

Transmission
Gearbox/no. of ratios: Mercedes-Benz (5 speeds, 4 synchronised plus reverse)
Clutch: Single dry plate

Chassis
Type: Tubular
Suspension: Parallel double wishbone, torsion bar, anti-roll bar front) swing axles, pivots, anti-roll bar (rear)
Dampers: Telescopic (front/rear)
Wheels: 600.16 (front) 700.16 (rear)
Tyres: Continental
Brakes: In-board drums (ATE)

Dimensions
Wheelbase: 2200 mm/ 2130 mm/2350 mm according to circuits
Tracks: 1330 mm (front) 1358 mm (rear)
Dry weight: 720 kgs
Fuel tank capacity: 200 litres

Raced from Argentina to Italy.

a free passage for the emergency services to intervene and to facilitate the exit and entrance of ambulances, firemen etc. Stopping the race would have created enormous traffic jams.

And so the event continued in a doom-laden ambience. And Fangio? Later on he invoked luck to explain how he avoided becoming involved in the accident. In hot pursuit of Hawthorn and not knowing that Mike had stopped he was coming up to lap Levegh when he saw the latter raise his arm in a last, despairing gesture either to warn of the impending crash or to show those behind a way through. "I saw the track clearing in front of me," he said, "a narrow corridor opened up which I drove through. Fate!" He got by intact missing

disaster by centimetres. The only mark on the car was a trace of green paint from Macklin's Austin Healey on the front and a broken headlight cover. It took Neubauer a long time to contact the Daimler-Benz management by telephone as all the lines were blocked. Finally, at 01h00 the two remaining SLRs - Fangio and Moss in the lead and Kling-Simon in fourth place - were officially withdrawn as a mark of respect. Or was it because the team wanted to avoid the cars being impounded at the end of the race? Whatever, they were loaded onto the transporters and driven back to Stuttgart by night.

The Le Mans accident cast a veil of grief and obloquy over motor racing. But in some ways it was the end of an era; that of a certain

• **96**_19ᵗʰ June 1955. An unusual shot of the start of the Dutch Grand Prix - except perhaps for Mercedes-Benz's rivals! Fangio is in no.18, Kling in no.12 and Moss in no.10 beside Musso's Maserati.
(Photo Daimler-Benz – William Huon archives)

• **97 and 98**_Just after the start and Musso has managed to split Fangio and Moss in their W 196s. Not for long, however, and Stirling soon passed the Maserati to latch on to his team-mate. The "Train" crossed the finishing line in that order with Moss only 3/10s behind his team leader. No doubt Mr. Neubauer, the station master, was a very happy man!

• **99**_16ᵗʰ July 1955: The four W 196s at the start of the British Grand Prix finished in the first four places, an exceptional result even by Mercedes-Benz standards.
(Photo Quadrant/LAT)

• **100**_Juan Manuel Fangio flat out at the wheel of his W 196 R during the British Grand Prix. Both driver and car represented the peak of perfection for their era.

insouciance where drivers, who had been through the war, bombing raids plus other calamities, accepted all kinds of risks to live their passion and one where constructors did not always do their utmost to make their cars safe. The organisers too had to rethink their priorities, as crowd safety was far from being top of the list. Often spectators were too close to the track and on certain occasions even ran across the road during a race. The immediate result of the crash was the cancellation of several events beginning with the Swiss, German and French Grands Prix. The first-mentioned went so far as to ban circuit racing completely on its territory.

A week after Le Mans the teams arrived at Zandvoort for the Dutch Grand Prix, which had not been cancelled, with the Le Mans disaster still in their minds. It was business as usual for Fangio and Moss who scored another double from Musso's Maserati. Next on the cards was the British Grand Prix on 16th July on the Aintree circuit. Mercedes duly notched up another win but this time it was Moss who took the chequered flag. It was a crushing victory for the Silver Arrows as the four cars entered finished in the first four places with Kling and Taruffi coming home third and fourth. It will never be known whether or not Fangio lifted off slightly to let Moss win his home Grand Prix. If he did he never said anything, which was totally in keeping with his character.

As a result of the cancellations the only remaining F1 event on the calendar was the Italian Grand Prix, which Fangio won, in a rather sick motor car, notching up his third F1 World Championship title. Moss retired and it was Taruffi who assured another Mercedes-Benz one, two.

In sports cars Fangio triumphed in the Swedish Grand Prix on the Kristianstad circuit followed by Moss giving the 300 SLRs another double. Victory in the Sports Car World Championship now hinged on the outcome of the Tourist Trophy on the Dundrod circuit in Northern Ireland on 17th September, an event that Mercedes-Benz had to win. They did and this time it was the Moss-Fitch 300 SLR that took the flag followed by Fangio-Kling and Simon-von Trips giving the Silver Arrows a triple. In Sicily Moss won again partnered by Peter Collins and Fangio and Kling scored another second place. Mercedes-Benz then withdrew from racing, not because of the Le Mans accident as has been wrongly stated, but because it had nothing left to prove. In addition, it allowed the company to concentrate its efforts on selling series production cars.

Aged forty-four Fangio thus won his third F1 World Championship from Stirling Moss. When he arrived home he gave serious thought to retiring for the first time in his life. ■

● **101**_9th August 1955: Fangio leads Moss home yet again as he takes the chequered flag to win the Swedish round of the Sports Car World Championship on the Kristianstadt circuit, a race not valid for the championship. *(International News photos/LAT)*

Chapter 12
1956
On the back of the Prancing Horse

In fact, politics were to throw a spanner into Fangio's plans for retirement. In September 1955 Peron was obliged to abdicate following the failure of his economic policies allied to the fact that the State's coffers were empty. It was that or civil war. He found refuge in Franco's Spain. While awaiting so-called elections a provisional government was set up and its first decision was to freeze the assets of hundreds of companies and private individuals for 150 days during which the people in question had to prove the legitimacy of their enrichment during the Peron years. If unable to do so their assets would be confiscated. While Argentina was in the throes of this upheaval Fangio was competing in the Venezuelan Grand Prix for Sports Cars in Caracas on 6th November in a Maserati 300 S. It was his first post Mercedes-Benz race and he won. His victory, however, led to a bitter dispute with Maserati as the Italian constructor wanted to keep the solid gold cup that went with victory. This incident led to an acrimonious break between the Argentinean and the Trident Company. Not knowing what would be the outcome of the 150 days moratorium on his finances Fangio was forced to drive for another year. But with which team?

The 250F Maserati was looking increasingly competitive and the company had just signed Stirling Moss as no.1 driver with Jean Behra in the no.2 spot and young Italian Cesare Perdisa as no.3. Ferrari was at a crossroads. In the summer of 1955 Lancia had run out of money and had signed over to Enzo Ferrari no fewer than six D 50s plus spare engines, gearboxes, tools etc. In addition, Ferrari as standard-bearer of the Italian

car industry had also received a big cheque from Fiat. In Italy racing was a national venture and a major commercial investment for the Turin company, which, over the years, bought up Ferrari, Lancia, Alfa Romeo and Maserati.

In that era Ferrari was still a small independent make with a couple of hundred staff and an output of approximately the same number of hand-built cars per year. Its founder, Enzo Ferrari, reigned as a kind of benevolent (occasionally!) despot over a factory and competitions service that was rudimentary in nature. To drive for the mythic Scuderia symbolised by the Prancing Horse was the dream of every driver and for those who did it was an honour. Enzo Ferrari was used to his drivers obeying him unquestioningly, not making the slightest comment about the cars entrusted to them and above all meekly accepting the terms of their contracts and payment. So when he asked Fangio to join the Scuderia he was somewhat taken aback to discover that the latter dealt through a manager! The man in question was a self-proclaimed but nonetheless redoubtable businessman called Marcello Giambertone. In addition, he was a former race organiser and thus knew the racing milieu like the back of his hand. When Ferrari met Giambertone and Fangio he had already announced his driver line-up for 1956, namely, two Italians, Eugenio Castellotti and Luigi Musso, a Spaniard, Alfonso de Portago and an Englishman, Peter Collins who were joined on an occasional basis by Olivier Gendebien from Belgium and moustached Frenchman, Maurice Trintignant. During the meeting Fangio smiled and barely spoke apart from the odd

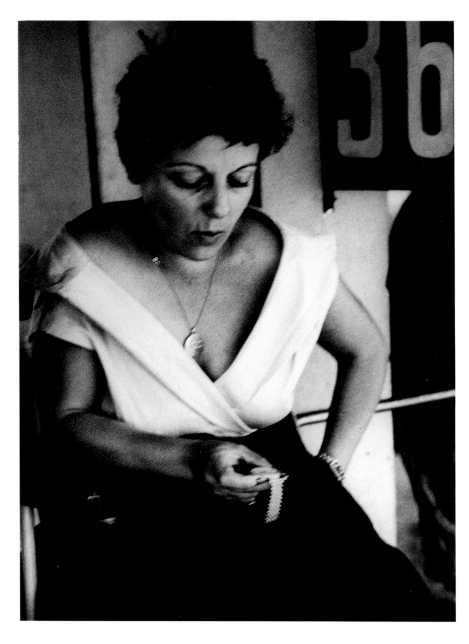

● **103**_22ⁿᵈ January 1956:
Beba, Fangio's companion,
times his climb back to victory
in the Argentinean Grand Prix
after he took over Musso's car.
(Photo Associated Press – LAT)

technical choices reduced the efficiency and homogeneity of the D 50s. The most visible change was in the flanks where the side-mounted pontoons were integrated into the bodywork. Originally, the Lancia's side tanks were separate from the body but on the Lancia-Ferrari they were located in the tail although many different layouts were tested during the races. Another innovation was the fitting of a de Dion rear axle. Overall these impressive looking cars were very competitive. With Nello Ugolini having gone to Maserati Eraldo Sculati took over the job of team manager.

The first round of the championship, the Argentinean Grand Prix, was held in Buenos Aires on 22ⁿᵈ January. The Ferrari drivers found themselves up against a Maserati team strengthened by the return of Gonzalez plus Mike Hawthorn who had not found a regular drive. Fangio set pole from Castellotti and Musso but his main challenge came from Gonzalez and Moss in their Maseratis. After Froilan retired Fangio took over Musso's car as his own was hit by fuel feed problems. The end of the race saw a battle royal between himself and his former team-mate with victory going to the Argentinean despite a brief off-course excursion. But once again Ugolini lodged a protest against "Bandylegs" claiming that he had been helped to restart by a push from some spectators. Now trying to have Fangio disqualified in his home country was more an exercise in wish-fulfilment than a realistic appraisal of the situation and the volatile Italian's protest was quickly thrown out. Juan Manuel had to share the eight points for victory with Musso but he also set the fastest lap adding another to his tally.

Not all of today's F1 fans are necessarily aware of how the Ferrari myth was born, as it owes a lot to the performance of the red cars in endurance events, which tested both men and machines to the limit. The modern era, epitomised by Schumacher and Ferrari's exclusive works involvement in F1, is not comparable to the 50s and 60s when the Scuderia competed in every form of racing. The drivers too did not limit themselves exclusively to the F1 World Championship and took part in other events. In early 1956 the Scuderia entered cars for a couple of sports car races before returning to Europe: first of all the Buenos Aires 1000 kms on 29ᵗʰ January in which Fangio shared a 4.9 litre Ferrari 410 with Castellotti. They led for a long time until the Italian hit a dog (!) losing several places. The Argentinean did another of his miracle comeback drives and retook the lead, but on lap 89 out of 106, the Ferrari's transmission went handing victory to the Moss-Menditeguy Maserati 300 S. Next on the calendar was the Sebring 12 Hour race in Florida on 24ᵗʰ March.

monosyllable. Ferrari could get little else out of him and had to deal with the inflexible Giambertone. He agreed a contract for his client that included a basic salary of twelve million liras, a first for a Ferrari driver, plus a 50/50 split of starting and prize money plus several other fringe benefits. It was a bitter pill for Ferrari to swallow but he signed all the same having remarked earlier to Fangio, "I know you're very expensive but I need you!"

In Maranello the Squalos were shelved and their creator, Aurelio Lampredi, went to Fiat. The 1956 cars, initially christened Lancia-Ferraris and then Ferraris were in fact, modified Lancia D50s. Their designer, Vittorio Jano, rejoined Maranello at the same time as his cars but a new engineer, Carlo Chiti, would gradually take his place and his

P. MÉNARD

Designer: Vittorio Jano

Engine

Make/type: Lancia D 50
Number of cylinders/layout: V8 (front)
Cubic capacity: 2489 ccs
Bore/stroke: 80 x 62 mm
Compression ratio: 11.5:1
Max. Power: 260 bhp
Max. revs: 8000 rpm
Block: alloy
Carburettors: 4 double barrel Solex
Distribution: 4 overhead camshafts
Number of valves per cylinder: 2
Ignition: 2 magnetos (Marelli)
Number of plugs per cylinder: 2

Transmission

Gearbox/no. of speeds: Lancia-Ferrari transversal (5)
Clutch: Dry, single plate Lancia-Ferrari

Chassis

Type: tubular
Suspension: Double wishbone plus stabiliser (front)
De Dion axle (rear)
Dampers: Hydraulic, leaf-spring (front & rear)
Tyres: Engelbert 550.16 (front) 700/16 (rear)
Brakes; Lancia-Ferrari drums in the wheels

Dimensions

Wheelbase: 2280 mm
Tracks: 1320 mm (front & rear)
Dry weight: 650 kgs
Fuel tank capacity: 200 litres

Used from Argentina to Italy.

This time there were no problems and the Ferrari duo took the chequered flag in their 860 Monza ahead of the Musso-Schell 3.5 litre Monza giving the Scuderia a double that augured well for the Manufacturers' Championship. On 29th April the Ferraris filled the first five places in the Mille Miglia run in pouring rain with victory going to Castellotti in his 290 MM from Collins-Klemantaski, Musso in an 860 Monza and Fangio in a 290 MM. Into fifth came Gendebien-Washer in a 250 GT Berlinetta winning the GT category. At the finish Juan Manuel said that he felt like he'd been driving for twelve hours sitting in a cold bath! In fact, a last-minute modification to the cockpit resulted in his legs being drenched by cold water each time he braked and he finished the event with his fingers completely frozen.

All great drivers can screw up a race during their career despite having a competitive car and all the right equipment. Senna, for example, did just this in the 1991 Spanish Grand Prix and Fangio did the same in Monaco in 1956. He arrived in the Principality as hot favourite after his non-championship wins in Buenos Aires on 5th February and Syracuse on 15th April even if he had retired in the Daily Express Trophy at Silverstone on 6th May. The clutch on his Lancia-Ferrari went and he took over Collins's car only to have exactly the same thing happen. In Monaco he was quickest in practice in 1m 44s ahead of Moss 1m 44.6s and Castellotti's Lancia-Ferrari in 1m 44.9s. On the second row were Behra and Schell in their Maseratis in 1m 45.3s and 1m 45.6s respectively. Moss, on top of his form

• **104**_The cover of the May 1956 issue of the magazine "L'Automobile." On the eve of the Monaco Grand Prix the magazine carried the story of the world champion's career as he had visited Paris and agreed to be interviewed and photographed. The cover photo was taken without a car and the steering wheel and column were stuck in the grass in the Bois de Boulogne!
(Christian Moity archives)

• **105**_During practice for the German Grand Prix Fangio chats with Collins and de Portago under the watchful eye of Eraldo Sculati, the Ferrari team manager.
(Christian Moity archives – D.R.)

that day, made a blinding get-away and immediately pulled out a big lead over everybody including Fangio. For once the Argentinean lost his legendary cool and spun at Sainte Dévote in his pursuit of the Englishman. Musso tried to avoid him as did Schell's Vanwall and both ended up in the straw bales retiring on the spot. Fangio continued the race in fifth place in a rather battered car while Moss was now even further ahead. Castellotti's Lancia-Ferrari stopped with broken transmission putting the Argentinean into fourth behind Behra and Collins. He quickly disposed of the Frenchman and closed in on his team-mate who let him through. But then his car began to show signs of wear and tear especially as Fangio had driven in a style that was the complete antithesis of his usual one bouncing off kerbs and hitting the wall in the Bureau de Tabac corner on lap 32. On lap 40 he stopped to have

the brakes and clutch adjusted and Castellotti took over. Collins was now back in second but just after half-distance he was brought in and the reigning world champion took over his car. He set off in hot pursuit of the two Maseratis Behra, back in second, and Moss. On lap 63 now driving in his usual impeccable style, he passed the Frenchman and tried his best to close the gap to Stirling fifty-two seconds ahead. Fangio threw all his reserves into the chase setting the fastest lap in 1m 44.4s, a speed of 108.448 km/h and at the finish the two were separated by only 6.1 seconds. It was a good day for Maserati thanks to the Englishman's victory and Behra's third place. The Frenchman was in the lead in the world championship with 10 points from Moss with nine and Fangio with eight as he had to share the points with Collins for second and with Castellotti for fourth.

The Monaco result was to weigh in the balance at the end of the season as well as posing a few questions about the Scuderia's sporting policy. Was it to make sure that one of its drivers (no matter who) would be crowned world champion or was it to privilege Fangio whose salary and status was that of a no.1 driver, thus ensuring a return on its investment? Had the latter simply taken advantage of Collins's stop, and the regulations? Between lap 40 when the Argentinean stopped and Castellotti went out in his car and lap 54 when he himself rejoined in Collins' what went on in the Ferrari pit? Did Giambertone twist Eraldo Sculati's arm? Did Fangio have his say in the decision? Was Enzo

Ferrari consulted? We will see further on that the outcome of the world championship was decided behind the scenes at Monza raising just as many questions. Did what happened in Monaco on 13th May mean that the decision had already been taken?

After the Nürburgring 1000 kms where he again shared an 860 Monza with Castellotti (second behind the Moss-Behra Maserati) Fangio arrived at Spa-Francorchamps for the Belgian Grand Prix on 3rd June. Once again he set a blindingly quick pole position in 4m 9.8s from Moss in 4m 14.7s and Collins in 4m 15.3s. Maybe it was his way of saying he was still a force to be reckoned with after his Monaco performance. In

• **106 and 107_**
3rd June 1956: Two shots of Fangio in his Lancia-Ferrari on the Spa-Francorchamps circuit during the Belgian Grand Prix. In the first he begins the climb up the Eau Rouge Raidillon and in the second he has reached the top. He led the race for 24 laps until the transmission broke.

● **108**_1st July 1956: An atmospheric group shot at the foot of the control tower just before the start of the French Grand Prix on the Reims circuit showing the light-hearted camaraderie that existed between the drivers of that bygone era. From left to right: Mike Hawthorn, Fangio, de Portago (half-hidden) Castellotti, Collins, Moss and Gendebien. Note that all the Ferrari drivers are wearing a black armband in homage to Dino Ferrari, Enzo's son, who died the day before. *(Christian Moity archives)*

● **109 and 110**_Two shots of the A.C.F Grand Prix. The leading Lancia-Ferraris of Fangio (10), Castellotti (12) and Collins (14) are caught by Harry Schell's Vanwall. In the first photo the English car can just be seen in the Muizon curve and in the second the Franco-American has almost caught the Italian cars as he brakes for Thillois.

typical Spa rain Moss made another of his lightning starts while Fangio was slow off the grid. Stirling stayed in front until lap 6 when Juan Manuel overtook him at Stavelot. The rain had stopped and the lap record was broken time and again. On lap 24 after Moss's Maserati had lost a wheel and he had taken over Perdisa's Fangio retired with broken transmission. Finally, victory went to Peter Collins who scored a totally deserved maiden world championship win. Into second having passed Behra's Maserati came Belgian, Paul Frère, an amateur in the true sense of the word after a great drive in a Lancia-Ferrari. He remembers the race with pleasure: "I was a last-minute replacement for Musso at Spa in 1956. He had broken his arm at the 'Ring the previous Sunday and Ferrari asked Sculati to contact me. I hesitated and first of all said no. I did not come to the first practice session and in the second I tested the car under pretext of writing an article in a newspaper about it. Finally, I gave in to temptation and I've never regretted my decision as I came second. The Lancia-Ferrari was the best F1 I've ever driven. Fangio? He was capable of surpassing himself in an amazing way. I saw him do it on two occasions: the first was of course on the Nürburgring in 1957 in a Maserati but at Spa in 1956 in the Lancia-Ferrari he was 3 seconds a lap quicker than Collins and Castellotti in the same cars and neither of them exactly hung about!"

In the French Grand Prix at Reims Fangio again scored but only three points for fourth place. Peter Collins won his second Grand Prix by a whisker (3/10s from Castellotti) well ahead of Behra with Fangio 5.2s behind the Frenchman. So what happened? Let Christian Moity, the famous French journalist, who was at the race tell the story (see insert overleaf).

In the provisional championship ratings after the French race Fangio was third with 13 points just behind Behra with 14 and Collins in the lead with 19. Moss was fourth with 12 just behind his former team-mates. The next event on the calendar was the British Grand Prix on the Silverstone circuit. Moss put on a dazzling display in front of his home crowd and grabbed pole in his Maserati with a lap in 1m 41s. This was a full second quicker than Fangio and two more than Hawthorn in the BRM and Collins. Behind on the

• **111**_Christian Moity with Fangio during a retrospective on the Charade circuit. The latter is looking at an article in Auto Passion about his museum in Balcarce.
(Photo Christian Bedeï)

Christian Moity:
" Reims 1956, one of his greatest races. "

"That day he really drove like a bat out of hell. We had just heard that Dino, Enzo Ferrari's son, had died the day before. The Ferrari drivers and mechanics wore a black armband. There were five Lancia-Ferraris at the start: Fangio, Castellotti, Collins, Gendebien and De Portago. In addition Collins was in the lead in the championship, which created a pretty steamy atmosphere, as it was a question of the triumph of the young wolves about to eat the leader of the pack! I don't really think that Enzo, as was rumoured, really wanted to favour Collins or any other young driver and to put Fangio at a disadvantage. He just wanted to prove that his cars were the best and that different drivers, even youngsters, could win in them. During practice Fangio destroyed all his rivals as he was the only one not to lift off in the long curve at Gueux after the pits straight. You could hear this clearly as the engine note of the V8 Lancia remained constant. He also stamped his territory by setting pole in 2m 23.3s a speed of 208.577 km/h which beat his 1954 best in the Mercedes-Benz. Castellotti in second got round in 2m 24.6s and Collins in 2m 24.9s in third. Then when he came back to the Ferrari pit saying that the car tended to jump out of fifth gear and that he had been obliged to hold the steering wheel in one hand through the corner and the gear lever in the other everybody was astounded! In the race he again put on a superb display and although Collins and Castellotti were initially ahead he passed them both on lap 3 and led until lap 39 opening up a comfortable gap over his team-mates. There were five Ferraris in the first five places and they thought they had the race wrapped up. However, Schell in his Vanwall caught them due mainly to a misunderstanding. The Scuderia team manager thought he was a lap behind but in fact he had taken over from Hawthorn, was on the same lap and was now right behind the three leading Ferraris. Fangio reacted immediately and pulled away but he then had to pit to have a leak in the fuel gauge repaired as petrol was spraying into his face. He lost two minutes. Castellotti and Collins took advantage of their team leader's misadventure, as did Behra. But the world champion went out with the bit between his teeth and cut his way back up through the field to a fourth place finish. Had there been another lap he would have swallowed Behra. Last time round as in Monaco he set the fastest lap in 2m 25.8s a speed of 204.981 km/h. Even though he did not win that day I still think it was one of his greatest races."

second row were two Vanwalls driven by Schell and Gonzalez specially flown to England by the English constructor. Hawthorn shot to the front at flag fall using the incredible acceleration of the torquey 4-cylinder BRM engine where he was joined by the second Bourne car in the hands of Tony Brooks known as the 'Flying Dentist!' Fangio had to work very hard to match the green cars' speed and after passing Brooks he spun on lap 8 and found himself back in sixth place. Moss in third managed to get past the BRMs both of which retired: Hawthorn's with broken transmission and Brooks' after a big accident followed by a fire from which Tony was lucky to escape almost unscathed. This allowed Fangio up to fourth place and when Collins and Salvadori ran into trouble the Argentinean found himself second behind Moss. Stirling then hit ignition trouble losing over a minute in the pits and finally retired with six laps to go. Thus, Juan Manuel scored his only British Grand Prix victory from Collins who had taken over de Portago's car.

The circus then set off for the Nürburgring theatre of the German Grand Prix on 5th August. By now the Argentinean had asked for and been given a second mechanic, Cassani, who was personally allocated to his car. Fangio set pole in 9m 51.1s (one second slower than his 1954 time in the Mercedes). He was followed by Collins in 9m 51.5s and Castellotti in 9m 54.4s, these three being the only drivers to break the 10-minute barrier. Moss could do no better than 10m 3.4s which was good enough to put him on the front row with the three Ferraris. This time the reigning world champion simply walked away from his rivals and on lap 2 he beat Hermann Lang's record set in 1939 in the W 163 Mercedes-Benz. Collins matched his pace for a while before going off while Moss managed to get with in thirteen seconds of him by lap 13 (out of 22) but to no avail. Juan Manuel took the chequered flag with forty-seven seconds in hand over the Englishman having left the lap record at a staggering 9m 41.s a speed of 141.189 km/h. He came away from

Germany with another nine points in his pocket (8 for victory plus 1 for fastest lap). Now aged forty-five he was still able to see off the young wolves like Moss, Castellotti and Collins with consummate ease even if occasionally they managed to get within sniffing of his rear wheels! The German race was one of his best wins but little did he know that the following year he was to score a victory on the same circuit, which ranks among the greatest in F1 history.

Before the Italian Grand Prix on the Monza circuit, the final round of the championship, Fangio had 27 points, five more than Collins and Behra both on 22 and Moss with 19. That year only the best five results were taken into consideration for the attribution of the title so in theory anyway each of these three drivers was in with a slight chance. Moss and Behra were the obvious adversaries but what would happen if Collins was in a position to win the race? How would the Scuderia react?

And as fate would have it this very situation arose in the race. As usual Ferrari pulled out all the stops for Monza and entered five cars for Fangio, Collins, Castellotti, Musso and de Portago with a sixth foreseen for beginner Wolfgang von Trips from Germany. Maserati also brought along five cars for Moss, Behra, Villoresi, Maglioli and Francesco Godia from Spain who had finished fourth at the 'Ring. Gordini, Vanwall and Connaught each entered three cars and there were another five private Maserati 250 Fs.

In practice Fangio again set pole in 2m 42.6s from Castellotti (2m 43.4s) and Musso (2m 43.7s). They were followed by veteran Piero Taruffi's Vanwall and Moss and Behra in their Maseratis. On lap 1 Juan Manuel came round in third place behind the two Italians: he was followed by Collins, Schell and Moss. Schell used the Vanwall's straight-line speed to power past both Collins and Fangio and set off after the leaders. As Fangio had foreseen the tyres on

• **112**_14th July 1956: Fangio at work! Here he throws the Lancia-Ferrari into a gentle drift combining precision and elegance. Although he was ill he won the British Grand Prix putting himself back in the title chase following his fourth place at Reims where he was slowed by a defective fuel gauge.

Castellotti and Musso's cars were unable to cope with the pounding they received especially on the banking's bumpy surface on which the Ferraris were exceeding the 270 km/h mark. They stopped to have them changed and into the lead went Moss with Fangio and Schell right on his tail in a typical Monza slipstreamer. On lap 8 the Argentinean hit the front but he was almost immediately repassed by the Maserati and the Vanwall. He decided to bide his time to see how things would develop but on lap 19 he was forced to stop with a broken steering arm. He got out of his car and after it had been repaired Castellotti went back out in his place. At half-distance Moss was in the lead from Schell, Musso and Collins with little to choose between

them. Fangio, though, was standing in front of the Ferrari pits clearly awaiting something. In came Musso to have a wheel changed. He was asked to hand over to the reigning world champion but refused. A little later Collins, now in third as Schell had retired, pitted for the same reason. When asked he offered his car to Fangio thus sacrificing his own chances of winning the title. This was obviously what the Argentinean had been waiting for and he went out in third place behind Musso. The Italian soon retired putting Juan Manuel into second. Moss, who drove a brilliant race setting a new lap record, went on to win owing his victory to Piotti as the

• **115 and 116**_The turning point in the Italian Grand Prix and the world championship shown on the front cover of the British magazine, Autosport, as Peter Collins hands over his Lancia-Ferrari to Fangio thus throwing away his own chances of winning the title. In the upper shot Fangio leads Collins and a Maserati during the race.

latter placed his Maserati behind the Englishman's, which had run out of fuel, and pushed it to the pit lane entrance! Fangio came home second chalking up his fourth world championship title with 33 points (30) from Moss 28 (27) and Collins 25. The three points he scored in the Monza race were enough to tip the scales in his favour. Although he was once again given a triumphant reception by his fellow-countrymen Fangio well knew that his 1956 season had not been the most glorious of his career. While he had driven some brilliant races the way he had won had left a bitter taste in his mouth. That was why he wanted to finish on a high note. ∎

SEPTEMBER 7, 1956

AUTOSPORT 1/6

EVERY FRIDAY

Vol. 13   No. 10

BRITAIN'S MOTOR SPORTING WEEKLY

Chapter 13
1957-1958
His swan song

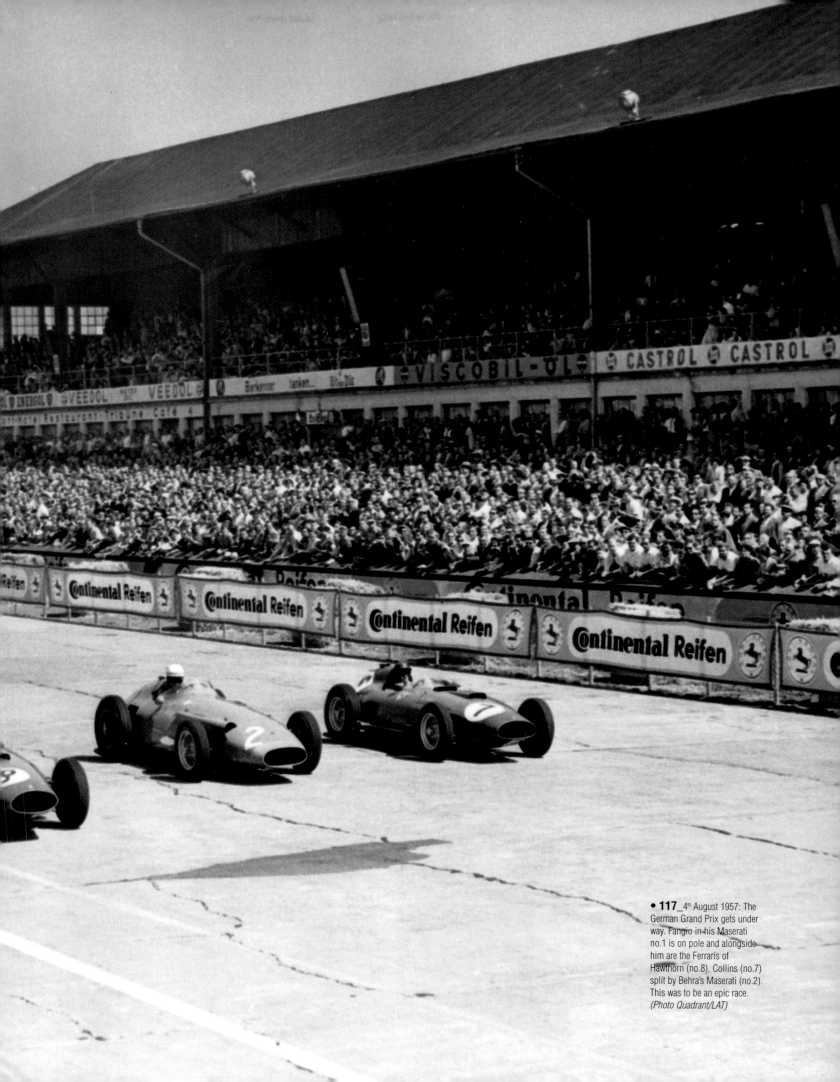

• **117**_4th August 1957: The German Grand Prix gets under way. Fangio in his Maserati no.1 is on pole and alongside him are the Ferraris of Hawthorn (no.8), Collins (no.7) split by Behra's Maserati (no.2). This was to be an epic race. *(Photo Quadrant/LAT)*

Fangio drove his last race for Ferrari on 11th November 1956, the Sports Car Grand Prix in Caracas, Venezuela. He was at the wheel of an 860 Monza and finished second. In December Enzo Ferrari announced his driver line-up for 1957: it included Collins, Hawthorn, Musso, Castellotti, Perdisa, de Portago, Trintignant, von Trips and Gendebien. And Fangio? Ferrari told the press, "unfortunately, we don't have the money to pay him". In fact, the latter had not at all appreciated the way in which Ferrari and Sculati had treated him and recontacted Omer Orsi, the Maserati boss, and his chief engineer, Guerrino Bertocchi. Fangio's aim was obviously to beat the Ferraris into a cocked hat and he reached a friendly agreement with Orsi sealed with a handshake on the basis of sharing starting and prize money 50/50. This was exactly what Ferrari had proposed a year earlier to Fangio and Giambertone but to no avail. Maserati had a new version of the 250F developed with the help of the engineer, Alberto Massimino, which was good enough to enable the Argentinean to beat the Ferraris. In addition, a new V12 engine was also available should the straight 6 not prove powerful enough. It produced an extra 40 bhp but was also heavier and made the car more difficult to drive. Joining Fangio and Jean Behra – who re-signed - were Harry Schell and Carlos Menditeguy. Moss threw in his lot with Vanwall but reserved the right to race for Maserati in the sports car championship for which the firm had developed the ultimate weapon, the 4.5 litre 420 bhp V8 450S.

The season kicked off as usual in Argentina with the national Grand Prix on 13th January on the Buenos Aires Autodromo. For once Fangio (1m 43.7s) was not on pole as he was pipped in

the closing minutes of practice by Stirling Moss in one of the three works Maserati 250 Fs (due to Vanwall's last-minute withdrawal) with a lap in 1m 42.6s. Fangio's enormous popularity did not exactly help crowd control and the spectators invaded the track sitting on the verges so the start was given in chaotic conditions. Moss's throttle linkage let him down and Behra went to the front followed by Castellotti and Fangio. After a skirmish between Behra and Eugenio Collins took up the lead on lap 11. Both the Englishman and the Italian were fated to retire (broken clutch plates in both cases) leaving Fangio, who has passed Behra, in first place where he stayed until the chequered flag leading home a Maserati one, two, three, four as behind himself and the Frenchman came Menditeguy and Schell. Fifteen days later he won the non-championship Buenos Aires Grand Prix confirming both his own scintillating form and the potential of his car. Between the two F1 races Moss and Fangio teamed up for the Buenos Aires 1000 kms in a Maserati 450 S. Moss did the first stint and was in the lead when he handed over to Fangio. The big Maserati blew the Ferraris off until its transmission went on lap 58 out of the 90 scheduled for the race.

This year there was another race on the Latin-American calendar, the Cuban Grand Prix on 25th February on the El Malecon city circuit in Havana. Fangio scored an easy victory in a 300 S Maserati little knowing that in 1958 he would make the headlines in the same event but for a very different reason. Then it was down to Florida where he was shared a Maserati 450 S with Behra in the Sebring 12 Hours which the Franco-Argentinean pair won giving the big Maserati its maiden victory.

"My seat began to move"

In Angouleme in 1987 Fangio in an interview for the magazine "Fanauto" described what it was like to live this race from the inside thirty years earlier.

"I was never a spectacular driver. I always drove within my limits taking as few risks as possible. But that day I really had to go for it. It's certainly the most spectacular race that I ever drove both for the spectators and myself. In the last lap the bolt holding the seat came out and it began to move. And I didn't have a seat belt! So on this roller coaster of a circuit I jammed my legs against the flanks of the bodywork bruising them in the process."

"Were you afraid during the last lap?"

• **126**_Fangio in the Karussel in hot pursuit of Collins and Hawthorn.
(Photo Quadrant/LAT)

" (Calmly) No, no you're too concentrated to be afraid. I took risks all right but I'd still say with a small safety margin. You can lose a lot of time on the straights. On the last straight there's a section which crosses a bridge. On the downward slope there you have to turn to the left a little and you have to brake just before the hump to take up the line. I was already well over on the left, foot hard down on the accelerator, the car was hopping about and in that era there was no guardrail just a hedge. Having taken off the car landed just beside the hedge and I said to myself: 'Well, that worked', so I did the same thing every lap and gained a lot of time. Normally all that downhill stretch is in second and I did it in third."

"You didn't try it in practice?"

• **127**_Fangio crosses the finishing line and can afford to relax at last. He has just won his fifth world championship to the frenzied applause of the crowd who know they've seen a race that will go down in history.

"No, it was a moment's inspiration during the race. I was lucky it worked; the car was very stable but I've no idea of how fast I was going there. Perhaps it's just as well!"

"I've got an image of you at the 'Ring in 1957. It's like a close up and you're hard at work, bare arms, polo neck, goggles, jaws hollowed by the speed";

"By concentration!"

Fangio finished second in the Pescara race and the Italian Grand Prix victory in both cases going to Stirling Moss's Vanwall. He won his fifth and last title with a total of 40 points from Moss (25), Musso (16) and Hawthorn (13). These figures give an idea of his domination in 1957, a result that is all the more impressive as he was forty-six at the time!

Italy was not the end of the season for him as on 27th October he drove his Maserati 250F to fourth place in the non-championship F1 Moroccan Grand Prix that would be included on the calendar the following year. In December he raced a Maserati 300 S in two events in Brazil in

South America, one on the Sao Paulo circuit and another a week later on the Boa Vista track in Rio de Janeiro. He won both adding two more victories to his mind-boggling string of results.

On 19th January 1958 the five times world champion drove for almost the last time in front of his home crowd. Fittingly enough the race was the Argentinean Grand Prix on the Buenos Aires circuit and guess who set pole? Why Fangio, of course and it was the last time that a Maserati would achieve this feat in an F1 Grand Prix. Behind him came his friends Hawthorn and Collins in their Ferraris. In the race itself Fangio took the lead and the threat to him came not

• **128**_On the rostrum Fangio's face shows the strain of going flat-out on the Nürburgring. Collins' smile is tinged with admiration while Mike Hawthorn's face wears a completely flummoxed expression!

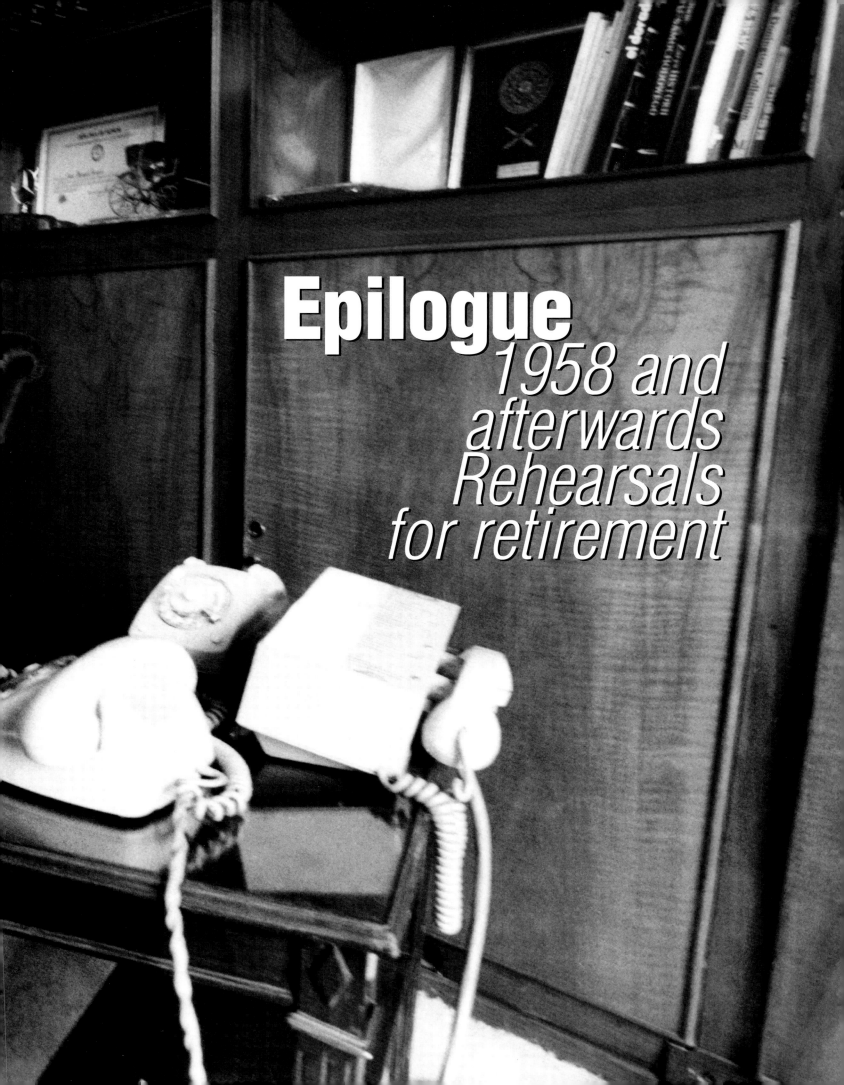

Epilogue
1958 and afterwards Rehearsals for retirement

The agreement between Fangio and Maserati stated that he could drive the new 250F "Piccolo" in four Grands Prix of his choice. After Reims as related at the beginning of this book the five-times world champion made up his mind to quit. And there was no going back. He would never race again. One of the reasons was the technical problems posed by the Maserati, but there was another one, this time of a sporting nature. In 1958, the distance of the Grands Prix was reduced to around 300 kms or two hours depriving Fangio of one of his strong points, his incredible stamina. There was a psychological one too: better to hang up his helmet at the height of his glory than staying on and being beaten by the rising generation of drivers. And finally there was another and more personal one. Fangio had just turned forty-seven: he had no children but his parents were still alive and he was deeply attached to them. Dona Herminia and Don Loreto were old and suffering from ill health. In fact, at the start of the 1958 season the family doctor had told Fangio that they should be shielded from strong emotions so one can imagine the effect on them of his kidnapping, the accident in the race the following day and his attempts to qualify for Indianapolis and Monzanapolis. On that 6th July

Musso's fatal crash in front of him when the Italian was barely thirty-four must have helped trigger a decision that was already at the back of his mind. He was too old to risk his life anymore and to put his parents under pressure each time there was a race, a practice session etc. Also he reckoned he had tempted fate more than enough and it was better not to try and stretch his luck any further.

Less than a month later Peter Collins was killed at the Nürburgring on 3rd August without ever winning the world championship after having sacrificed his chances when he handed over to Fangio in 1956. In 1958, honours went to Mike Hawthorn who was deeply affected by the death of Collins whom he nicknamed "Mon Ami, Mate." He decided to give up racing and soon afterwards met his maker in a traffic accident on 22nd January 1959. On 1st August of the same year Jean Behra was killed on the "Avusrennen" and on 13th May 1960 Harry Schell died in an accident during practice on the Silverstone circuit. All these accidents only went to prove how right Fangio was when he decided to hang up his helmet and gloves and return to his aging parents, his brothers and sisters and his home town of Balcarce as well as his business interests in Buenos Aires.

Of course, he continued to lead a life that had little to do with the conventional idea of retirement. As he was in excellent health and used to travelling and also a very astute businessman, his affairs prospered. In particular, he became President of Mercedes-Benz Argentina and in the area of sport he reckoned that motor racing had given him a lot and he tried to return some of it in his own way. He was elected honorary president of the "Former Grand Prix Drivers' Club" in 1958 and the following year occupied the same post on the Argentinean Motor Sporting Commission. He was also invited to give the start to F1 Grands Prix on a regular basis. The first was in Italy in 1958 followed by the German Grand Prix on the 'Ring in 1961. His old friend Stirling Moss won it and his victory became part of motor racing legend just four years after the Argentinean's marvellous achievement. He also gave the start to the 1981 Argentinean Grand Prix where a young French driver called Alain Prost got to meet him. He was the Clerk of the Course of the 1971 Buenos Aires 1000 kms in which an Italian driver, Ignazio Giunti, was killed. He witnessed the collision and took the side of Frenchman, Jean-Pierre Beltoise, wrongly accused of causing the accident.

He was also asked to advise young, up-and-coming drivers. One was Argentinean Juan Manuel Bordeu who was introduced to him by a mutual friend in the early 60s. He helped him

contact European teams and Bordeu did some Formula Junior and GT races (in a Ferrari 250 GTO in particular) without showing real talent. His career was more or less ended by an accident at Goodwood. Young "Cacho" Fangio tried to use his name to launch his racing career: he was not Juan Manuel's son but that of his long-time girlfriend, "Beba" and his star waned as quickly as it had waxed. In the 80s and 90s a Fangio did make a name for himself in racing, Juan Manuel Fangio II. He was "Toto's" son and Juan Manuel's nephew. He raced in the USA with considerable success in sports prototypes notably in the Toyota-powered Eagles entered by Dan Gurney's All American Racers Team. He won the Sebring 12 Hours twice and also the IMSA Championship on two occasions.

Even though Fangio no longer raced he drove cars up to the 90s. In September 1958 he was at the wheel of a Maserati 250F on the Modena circuit for a film on his career sponsored by BP: he also made several appearances at historic events and races demonstrating different cars to the great joy of spectators of all ages. On the Dijon circuit he drove a Maserati 250F before the main race, the 1975 Swiss Grand Prix, and for the 50th anniversary of the Nürburgring in 1977 he got behind the wheel of a Mercedes-Benz W 196. The same year he drove an Alfa Romeo 159 in Montreux and 1978 saw him in a Mercedes-Benz W 196 at Angoulême.

● **136**_May 1990: Fangio met Ayrton Senna before the Monaco Grand Prix with whom he became good friends.

143

In 1982 aged seventy-one Fangio was admitted to a Buenos Aires hospital for a major heart operation, a quintuple bypass. He emerged smiling and confident that he still had several good years ahead of him. Argentina was going through a dark period in its history and Juan Manuel kept his political ideas to himself while expressing his faith in democracy. He still had a very personal dream to fulfil, the construction of a museum in Balcarce. In 1979, a commission was set up with the right backing to render a lasting homage to the Argentinean champion. An architect came up with plans for a museum that included a circular gallery inspired by the Guggenheim Museum of Modern Art (MOMA) in New York. These received Fangio's approval and he kept a weather eye on the construction of the museum to which he gave his personal collection of vehicles. He also received gifts of several of the cars in which he had forged his legend. The 'Negrita' and the Volpi-Chevrolet, restored by Fangio and his brother, were on show as was a replica of the Chevrolet coupe plus cars offered by constructors like Gordini, Alfa Romeo (Alfetta 159) and Mercedes-Benz (a W 196) among others. The museum was officially inaugurated on 22nd November 1988 in the presence of Fangio who, in his speech underlined the aim of the "Centro Technologico Cultura y Museo del Automovilismo Juan Manuel Fangio" as it was named. It was not to glorify the quintuple world champion but to encourage young people who wanted to pursue a career in motor racing and "to generate greater enthusiasm for a sport that did not seem to have any limits where speed was concerned, but whose basic values must be humanity, bravery, gallantry and honesty as one's life was at stake even if it is the car that triumphs." Wise words that many professional racing drivers would do well to meditate on.

Fangio was again to appear in public and he visited Europe in 1990 when the Pirelli album written by Stirling Moss was published. He went back to Stuttgart to Mercedes-Benz and attended the Monaco Grand Prix to promote the book. He said hello to Ayrton Senna with whom he became friends as the Brazilian sometimes opened up his heart to the sage from Argentina. Fangio was shattered by Senna's death at Imola on 1st May as Ayrton had phoned him shortly before his accident telling him about his uneasiness and the pressure he was under from his team.

• **137**_In 1990, Fangio was reunited with a replica of his Chevrolet coupe TC for the Pirelli album.
(Photo Pirelli)

• **138**_For the same book he posed
in the Alfetta 159, which Alfa Romeo
gave him for the Balcarce museum.
Sitting on the tyre is Mauro Povia,
his tyre fitter at Pirelli. Fangio never
forgot those who worked with him.
(Photo Pirelli)

The five-times world champion outlived Senna by about a year. His state of health suddenly deteriorated very quickly and the situation was not helped by the fact that he had been under dialysis for several years. On 15th July 1995 he was rushed to hospital in Buenos Aires where he died on 17th July at 4h40 just after his eighty-fourth birthday. He was buried in the Balcarce cemetery.

To paraphrase the Chinese sage Lao Tsu. Did Fangio dream his life or did he live a dream? He was a true believer who always thanked luck and remained very suspicious of politics throughout his long life. He was kind enough to write to us in the autumn of 1987 in reply to a question on his racing philosophy and on life in general. In answer he asked us to quote the great Spanish playwright, Pedro Calderon de la Barca (1600-1681) whose play "Life is a Dream" he liked very much. Here follows an extract in the form of a farewell:

"Man dreams what he is until he awakens.
The king dreams he's a king
And lives this fantasy:
He orders, disposes, governs;
But this borrowed glory
Leaves its trace in the wind
And death, a dire curse!
Soon changes him into ashes!
Why want to reign
Knowing that awakening
Brings the dream of death?
The rich man dreams of his riches
Which bring him but worries:
The poor man dreams he suffers
From his misery and distress:
He dreams up prosperity
Business, ambition
Insults, humiliation;
In this world for sure
Every one dreams who he is
But none understands it....
What is life? Madness
What is life? An illusion,
A shade, a fiction
Greatest happiness is found in the least of things,
For all of life is a dream
*And a dream's worth only a dream**

"Life is a Dream", Calderon de la Barca.